INVERNESS REMEMBERED V

Published By
New Century Publishing Group

The Inverness Courier

INVERNESS REMEMBERED
V

Compiled by Willie Morrison

The photographs in this book were sourced with the generous help of the people named below, who were kind enough to respond to our appeal for fascinating reminders of Inverness in bygone days.
Every effort has been made to ensure the information used is as accurate as possible.

Jeff MacLeod
Ted Murdoch
Leonella Longmore
Win MacKenzie
Marie Maciver
P Macpherson
Duncan Robertson
Marlene Lobban
Graham Spence
John Macdonald
Jock Hay
Anne C Mackintosh
Donald MacKechnie
Marjory Mackenzie
Anel Anderson
Mrs M MacDonald
Archie Fraser
Eleanor and David Mellis
Phyllis Mackenzie
Linda Law
Tony Hogg
James Pirrie
Peter Chisholm
A Edgar
Willie Shand
Angus Macdonald
Eileen Melrose
Iris MacLeod
Agnes Macrae
Alex Fridge
Fiona Macdonald
L A Riach
Mrs P Ross
Iain Cameron
Mrs Mary Nairne
Charles Macdonald
Sheila Burnett
Alister Paterson
Rory MacLeod
Donnie Mackintosh
Mary MacDonald
Catherine Harper
Maureen Smith
James Macpherson
Catherine Cascarino
Mrs S Mackenzie
Murdo Macleod
Sheila Macdonald
Sally MacKenzie
Mr and Mrs A Chisholm
Douglas Taylor
M B Corrance
Mrs Margaret Murphy
Mrs S Williamson
James Fraser
Hugh Grant
Robin Mackay
Patricia Neumann
M Kelly
Mary Nicoll
Marion Cooper
Christine McLoughlin
Stewart MacLennan
Alex MacLennan
Charles Crawford
R Ross
Willie Morrison

A Catalogue Record for this book is available from The British Library.

CONTENTS

INTRODUCTION

In our latest volume of Inverness Remembered, we look back once more to photographs from eras when, apparently, life was slower and more leisurely.

Or was it really?

Some of us, perhaps, see the past through rose-tinted spectacles, as the passage of time, combined with nostalgia, lends a patina of romance to these bygone decades or centuries. With age, this tendency often becomes more acute.

Life was certainly slower in those days, of course, as far as general communications were concerned, though it's worth noting that a century ago, the train journeys between Inverness and London or other major cities took only marginally more time.

For the wealthy few, existence might indeed have been more leisurely. However, the vast majority, if not in downright poverty, were only modestly endowed with worldly goods, and were forced to work harder, faster and longer than almost any counterparts today, while the wiser among them practised thrift as a matter of necessity. Benefits cheques were unknown, poor relief was often bestowed grudgingly at the whim of parish councillors, or from private charity, while the last resort for all too many was the poorhouse.

Few married women in Inverness of even a century ago worked for outside employers, except perhaps at casual menial tasks like occasional washing or cleaning for those who could afford to farm out their chores. According to the culture of the time, the married woman's place was in the home.

Until well after World War II, female teachers in Scotland, for example, generally had to resign their posts on marriage, and if they were employed, certainly by some local authorities, it was only on a casual basis, even as late as the 1950s.

These restrictions did not, however, save women in poorer circumstances from the drudgery of keeping homes,

frequently without proper sanitation or sufficient food, and striving to look after families on remittances from their husbands' generally frugal wages.

It seems, though, from contemporary records, that many ordinary folk of limited means, provided they had enough to live on, were indeed happier in the past, simply because their material expectations were rather less than those of today's population.

They didn't have television, or until the inter-war years even radio, constantly reminding them about that mythical other side of the fence where the grass was supposedly greener. The advent and growth of the movies possibly did fire the imaginations of many, and quicken the desire to move away from home, or do something other than the humdrum.

We have this year highlighted two particular citizens of bygone days from different ends of the town's social spectrum – a long-serving town clerk who also championed crofters' causes throughout the Highlands, and a remarkable mother, nurse and midwife, who delivered over 300 babies without a single fatality, besides bringing up 12 children of her own, after her husband died young.

Despite the name Inverness Remembered, in this year's volume there is a selection of pictures from an era a decade or two beyond living memory, taken from some very old souvenir photographic books of Inverness, dating from late Victorian or Edwardian times.

Older readers may well recognise most of the views as being not too different from those they knew in younger days, while some, happily, have remained very much as they were then, right to the present day.

MISTAKEN IDENTITY

The teacher on the left of the Inverness Technical High School class photograph from the mid-1950s, on page 85 of Inverness Remembered IV, was Duncan Gordon, who taught English, not the late Calum Cumming, who taught maths, Mr Cumming's wife Joyce has informed us. Mrs Cumming, who worked in the school office, recalls that both began teaching at the school on the same day. She also informs us that Charlie MacKenzie, who appeared in the photo of trophy-winning 7th Inverness Coy Boys' Brigade physical training team of 1949, sadly died in Canada in January of this year. In addition, Mrs Cumming has passed on all the names of the High School hockey team pictured on Page 51 of Inverness Remembered II. They are rear, from left: Mory Lumsden, Kath Bowman, Frances Fraser, Anne Shirra, Ella MacLean; front, from left: Isobel Kennedy, Margaret MacLean, Joan Urquhart, Rachel Douglas, Margaret Young, Joyce Rattray.

INVERNESSIANS LOOK BACK

Staff of High Street branch of the Bank of Scotland gathered in the Highland Club in 1959 to mark the retiral of manager Stirling Kirkland, sitting, centre. They are, rear, from left: G Kirk, L Macintosh, Miss P Pears, W Forsyth, I Fullerton, Miss J Hall, G Fraser, W Brunton; front, from left: Miss J Marshall, Miss C MacDonald, Miss M Fraser, H MacDonald, Miss F Dunbar.

This young man was hitching a lift home to Inverness from Aberdeen University one day in May 1967, when a passing journalist gave him a lift. Intrigued to learn that the student, Graham Spence, was so devoted to his girlfriend that he hitch-hiked home to Inverness every weekend to see her, the reporter thought it would make a good wee story. He posed this photograph of Graham beside the old A96 near the burgh, with the then fairly modest village of Balloch in the background. Graham, who now lives in retirement in Balloch, ended a distinguished career in education in 2007, after 17 years as rector of Millburn Academy, having previously served eight years as assistant director of education with Highland Regional Council. He married his girlfriend Helen, who sadly has since passed on.

This presentation photo, taken in December, 1987, in the Railway Club, Inverness, was passed on by retired railwayman Jock Hay, who is pictured here front, right, with the clock he received to mark his retirement as a diesel engine instructor. "There are very few in the picture left now," says Jock, who lives in Lochardil. Also receiving a presentation was David Fraser, front, left, from Tom Haggerty, the train crew manager at Inverness locomotive department. Rear, from left, are Alasdair Moore, Jock Macpherson, Bob Blaney, Kenny Campbell, Davie Irvine and Bobby Robertson. Sadly Bob Blaney, who had been ill but who had insisted on attending, died the next day.

John Macdonald had been on point duty in High Street one day in the summer of 1964 when a shop assistant reported a little boy of three or four who had been parted from his mother. The strapping but gentle 6ft 3in police officer is photographed here in Strothers Lane carrying the wee lad to the burgh police headquarters, at that time based at Farraline Park, in what is now the city library. Although John, from Melness, Sutherland, retired as a high-ranking officer of Northern Constabulary in 1994, many in the burgh remember him best as Big John or John the Bike, when he cycled around the east side of Inverness in his role as community officer, in the late 1960s and early 1970s. John, who never learned the boy's identity, would love to know where he is now and what became of him.

Three generations of Riachs, an Inverness family who owned a jewellers' business in Church Street from 1926-1953. They are, from left: Major Alex R Riach, who was made OBE for his services in the Great War, his grandson Alex J Riach, and his son James A Riach.

A group of Lovat Scouts taken at camp at Bruich, 12 miles from Inverness, probably in the 1930s. Judging from the campaign ribbons, the only Great War veteran is the corporal sitting cross-legged at the front.

Highland members of the Royal Observer Corps pictured at their Raigmore headquarters bunker in 1949. Sixteen-year old recruit Jane Smith, later Hamilton, is the lass pictured second left in the front row above. The photos were submitted by her sister, Agnes Macrae.

Inverness man Charlie Macdonald was a lance-bombardier in the Royal Artillery when he married Sylvia Morse at St Mary's Church in her native Tenby, Wales, in 1947, having already served five years in the army.
He later became a supervisor at Inverness Telephone Exchange. The couple, who lived for most of their married life in Swanston Avenue, Inverness, celebrated their golden anniversary in 2007.

Playtime at Kessock Road, 1962, from left, Kathleen Aitken, David Aitken, Sally, Margaret and Nancy Wood, Linda Mackenzie.

This photo, of railwaymen receiving 35-year service awards, taken in November 1975, at the Columba Hotel, Inverness, was also provided by Jock Hay (see page 9). In the picture are, rear, from left: Davie Mackay, Willie Ross, Alex Lewthwaite, Jacky Gordon, Jock McAngus, Peter Keil, Rory Macdonald, William Fraser; third row, from left: Tommy Dey, Tom Haggerty, Inverness stationmaster James D Watson, Ed Manson, John Mackenzie, Bob Taylor, Donald Mackenzie, Jock Hay, Willie Lobban, Jimmy Mackay; second row, from left: George Stewart, Sandy Sutherland, Donald "Dodo" Munro, John Fraser, Jimmy Smith, John G Munro, Jimmy Davidson, Donnie Maclennan; front row, from left: Davie Fraser, Adam Sutherland, William Davidson, Jock Glass, George Spence.

World War II was not far away when this carefree trio was snapped in Inverness in 1939. Christina Mackenzie is holding her little son Murdo's hand, as she walks with her sister Cathy Sim. The sisters' surname before marriage was Hoban.

The next batch of photos was contributed by retired electrician Archie Fraser, of St Ninian Drive, and his wife Marlene.

A young Alex Fraser, then a gas lamplighter employed by Inverness Town Council, tries out a penny-farthing cycle in Castle Wynd, where the lighting department was based. The identity of the other two people is unknown, as is the ownership of the penny-farthing, although the man supporting the cycle was possibly a colleague.

These young telephonists were pictured taking advantage of the new rest room established in the telephone exchange in 1960.

Some of the staff of Inverness Telephone Exchange, pictured in the late 1950s, or early 1960s. They are, front, from left: Kathleen Rankin, Grace Fraser, Evelyn Sutherland; rear, from left: May MacDonald, Lilian Ross, Iris Davidson, Jean McMillan, Margaret Urquhart, Marlene McMillan, Isobel Urquhart, Nan Walker, Isobel Munro.

Gas lamplighter and part-time fireman Alex Fraser pictured initiating teenage apprentice John Macdonald into the mysteries of his trade.

Archie Fraser, who wasn't a 100 Club member, but was invited to join the party by his friend Donnie Mackintosh, recalls being quite awed by the adventure, which included a descent to the coal face. Archie is the impish lad second from the left, while beside him is Donnie, his arms around a smaller lad. The tall boy, third from right, rear row, is Leslie Hodge.

Members of an early Inverness judo club, coached by Stewart Chisholm, centre, rear row, pictured in 1956. A young Archie Fraser is third from the left, front row. The only other name he can remember is Alex MacCulloch, extreme left, front row.

A Remarkable Mother and Midwife

This Inverness couple were, if not wealthy, comfortably well off by the standards of their time, when the photo was taken in 1913.
Joe Davidson's smartly-cut suit, set off by a gold albert, advertised his calling as a tailor and clothier in Pumpgate Street.
His wife Isabella, also suitably if perhaps a little severely clad, was a highly-respected nurse and midwife in Merkinch, where Joe and Isabella lived at Lower Kessock Street.
Tragically their circumstances were to change drastically by the next year.
Joe not only enjoyed a good reputation in his chosen trade, but also as a footballer with Clachnacuddin Football Club, where in his youth he was reputedly one of the finest forwards the burgh had produced.
He acted as the club's trainer for five years, and remained a committee member until his sudden death from a brain haemorrhage in 1914, at the age of 41, leaving his wife to bring up their family of 12 on her own.
Despite her personal tragedy, brave Isabella didn't flinch, and continued to act as nurse and midwife, being credited with bringing over 300 Merkinch children into the world between 1912 and 1930 without a single fatality – a truly incredible feat for that era.
Her grand-daughter Phyllis Mackenzie, of Dochfour Drive, who submitted this photograph, says: "Mrs D, as she was known, could be called out at any time of the day or night, and helped countless families.
"She also set up a welfare project in a hall in Grant Street in the 1920s, showing mothers how to care for their babies and weighing and keeping charts of their progress before the days of the National Health Service.
"The hall was later known as the Welfare Hall and used for community activities, which Mrs D organised. The building still exists, though is no longer in use.
"Mrs D also worked for funeral undertakers D Chisholm & Sons, in her capacity as a nurse, to attend to the deceased, while local doctors often called for her services in a private nursing role," reveals Phyllis Mackenzie.
This truly remarkable mother and midwife died in May 1946, in her early 70s.

Bert Edgar, of Inverness bakery family Robert Edgar, is pictured in the Cummings Hotel, Inverness, in the 1950s, giving young farmers a talk on walking-stick making. The business was founded in 1901 in Church Street, Inverness, by Hawick baker Robert Edgar, who died in 1929, and was taken over by Nairn bakery Asher's in 1969.

Happy at the prospect of returning home, after a hard fortnight's training at Thetford Camp, Norfolk, in autumn 1969, were these fit young Inverness and district Territorial Army members of 51 Highland Volunteers, pictured just before leaving on their last day. Among those in the photo are well-known local bus driver Dave Scott, far left, who although now retired, still works the odd shift, and solicitor David MacNeill kneeling, right, who practised in Oban, first as procurator-fiscal, and later as a criminal lawyer, until shortly before his death in 2009.

Smiling faces of 3rd Inverness (Crown) Company, Boys' Brigade, pictured in the early 1950s. They are, rear, from left: J Guthrie, R Cameron, C Ross, M Macrae, W Fraser; middle row, from left: R Morrison-Smith, I Johnstone, M Fraser, B White, D Mellis, J Crawford, D Polson; front, from left: W Macintyre, A Coll, C Nairne, K Mackenzie, A Allan, unidentified.

It's 1967 and on the eve of his wedding day, electrician David Mellis is being subjected to a ritual "bridegroom's blackening" by his workmates, from left, Bill Ross, Charles Young and David Glass. The lads were then employed by electrical company B French, and were at that time working on the nurses' home at the Royal Northern Infirmary.

This carefree foursome was snapped in High Street in the late 1940s by a street photographer of the kind not uncommon in days when the average household did not own a camera. The girls are named on the back of the print merely as Sheena, Rena, Ann and Madeline.

The owners and staff of Bullock Brothers' garage in Tomnahurich Street, pictured in the early 1950s. In the photo, from left, are: Alisdair Bullock, co-proprietor, Taylor Bullock, Eck Morrison, Willie Bullock, co-proprietor with his brother Alisdair, and Taylor's father, Andrew Bullock, brother of Alisdair and Willie, who owned a cycle shop across the road, Don Morrison, Eck's brother. Alisdair and Willie later moved for some years to premises in Greig Street, before retiring. The car, registered AJS 59, is a Hillman Minx Mk V, produced by Rootes Brothers of Coventry between 1951 and 1953. This photo was submitted by Willie Bullock's daughter, Eileen Melrose.

A performance staged in the 1950s by Sheila Ross's School of Ballet. Sheila, who was the daughter of Provost Alan Ross, married Fred Kelly of the well-known Inverness gents' outfitters and still lives in Inverness. The prima donna in the lead role is thought to be Annelle Watson.

This picture, as the bold caption underneath states, is of Inverness Girls' Pipe Band, and was taken specially for a 1959 calendar produced as a fund-raiser for the band. Founded in the early 1950s, by former Cameron Highlander David Ross, it lasted until a couple of years before his untimely death in 1968, at the age of 51. His daughter Iris Macleod, a keen band member, who gave us the photo, recalls that the band raised funds for all its equipment, including instruments, uniforms and the drum-major's mace, which it donated to the Boys' Brigade when the band dissolved. In this photo are, rear, from left: Vera Chambers, Irene Kelman, Gladys Butchart, Moira Polson, Margaret Henderson, Eunice MacRae, Margaret MacReadie, Lillian Mackay, Catherine Montgomery; front, from left: Kathleen McGurk, Ann Henderson, Rachel Mackay, Evelyn MacKenzie, Iris Ross, Jean Webster, Sheila Reid, Ena Falconer, Pipe Major David Ross.

An early photo of Inverness Girls' Pipe Band, taken around 1951. Rear row, from left: Unidentified, unidentified, Betty Lockhart, David Ross, unidentified; front, from left: Sheila Mackintosh, Agnes Smith, Vera Chambers, Sheila Reid, Jessie Cumming, Iris Ross, Helen Flynn, unidentified.

Inverness Girls' Pipe Band was in its prime in 1958, when this photo was taken at Merkinch School Hall, where it practised. Rear, from left: Helen Flynn, Sheila Reid, Evelyn MacKenzie, Ena Falconer, Iris Ross, Lillian Skinner; middle row, from left: Pipe Major David Ross, Rachel Mackay, Kath McGurk, Lillian Mackay, Ann Henderson, Willie Mackay (tutor); front, from left: Irene Kelman, Vera Chambers, Gladys Butchart, Helen McKeddie, Margaret MacReadie, Margaret Henderson, Catherine Montgomery. *See also page 101.*

James Macpherson, of Dochfour Drive, had the misfortune to turn 18 at the start of one of the 20th Century's worst winters, and to be called up shortly after, in February 1947, to start his initial training course at the Cameron Barracks. By the time of the passing out parade, six weeks later, snow was still thick on the ground, as this photo shows. "We had no water in the barracks during the whole time," he recalls, "as the pipes were frozen. We had to get water from the cookhouse to wash in. But we still had to do our physical training outside in the snow in shorts. It was very cold." The squaddies are seen here with Company Sergeant Major Mulherne, who was reputed to have been goalkeeper for Caley FC in an earlier incarnation, Corporal Andy Roberts, from Kingussie, both of whom sport World War II campaign ribbons, and Lance-Corporal Bowker, a Mancunian, who had relatives in King Street, Inverness. James says he can't remember which was himself, but tells us there are several Inverness lads and many from the Highlands in the squad. He was subsequently sent to Catterick, to train as a tank radio operator, before being posted to Germany to serve with the 5th Inniskilling Dragoon Guards, at that time operating Cromwell tanks. "I quite enjoyed the army, but two years was enough," reflects James, who in civilian life worked successively in the planning departments of Inverness County Council, Highland Regional Council and Highland Council.

Bob Dingwall, pictured here by Inverness photographer Andrew Paterson in the smart uniform of a Queen's Own Cameron Highlander before marching off to the Great War, was luckier than many of his colleagues. At least he returned, but not unscathed, having lost an eye during his time in the trenches. After recuperation and demob, he became a postie. He married local lass Catherine Fraser and lived first in Macdonald Road, before settling at 98 Bruce Gardens, where the couple raised a family of three. He died in 1966 aged 71. His grandson Robin Mackay, who sent in this photo, recalls how as a party piece he used to take out his artificial eye and polish it.

Bob's daughter, Jessie Dingwall, known as Nettie, pictured here, aged 17, outside her home at 98 Bruce Gardens on 11 March 1937. She married, at 20, Donald Mackay, of Thurso origin, and was Robin's mother, but despite that, worked throughout her life, starting at Hugh Jack's well-known shop on The Exchange, approximately where Inverness tourist office is today.

A wartime studio photograph of the Dingwall family. The Royal Artillery lance-bombardier on the left is elder son Francis, with beside him his twin sister Jessie. Father Bob is in the centre, with his wife Catherine, seated, and younger son Bobby on the right. Bobby later served in the RAF, and he and his brother had a remarkably unexpected reunion in the Far East before their demob. Sadly all in this picture have since passed on.

Where today are all the bright young things in this picture, taken at Inverness Welfare League football dinner-dance at the Columba Hotel in December 1970? Many, we hope, will, in years to come, be able to point themselves out to their grandchildren. Christine McLoughlin, then Christine Chrystall, second row, far left, who sent it in, says: "I am not sure of all the names, but the people I do know are James Jarvie, Roger Anderson, Ian Mackintosh, Brian Mackintosh, James McBeth, Norman Glennie who was head boy at Inverness Royal Academy, Norma Taylor, Marsaili MacRae, Marianne McIntosh, Stewart Inglis and Yvonne McLennan." We also recognise, second row from rear, fourth from left, Hugh MacRae, who in those days played a prominent part in the affairs of Inverness Thistle FC, and was very helpful to members of the press.

This group of altar boys was taken outside St Mary's RC Church in Huntly Street around 60 years ago. In it are, rear, from left: Andrew Cameron, Peter Chisholm, Ronnie Ross; centre, from left: Gordon Richardson, Hugh Coyle, Victor Salvadori, Gordon Reilly; front, from left: Donnie Mackenzie, Sandy King, Terry Morrison, John Dailly, Alex MacLennan, Jack Ross.

French "onion johnnies" from Brittany were a familiar and welcome sight in the streets and suburbs of Inverness for many summers last century, until the early 1970s, when supermarkets and "progress" saw off the last of them. This photo, from the late 1950s, shows, from left, brothers Louis and Andre Chapalain, and their father Henri, all regular visitors to the town, but now sadly deceased.

Another photo of the Breton "onion johnnies" with their hosts at Dixie Villa, the old Customs House in Anderson Street where they stayed during their Highland tour. They had just received a visit from their abbe or priest (left) shortly before returning to their home community of Roscoff. Along with the priest, are, from left: Henri Chapalain, Margaret Stewart, who owned the house, Alex MacLennan, Louis Chapalain, Rose Ann MacLennan, Rose MacLennan, Claude Tanguey and Andre Chapalain.

Forty years ago these were the local politicians and their aides who ran Inverness Burgh, before local government in the Highlands gave way to one amorphous all-purpose authority covering the entire region. They are, from left: Town Officer Charlie Macrae, Baillie Robbie Grigor, Baillie Bill Fraser, Town Clerk John R Hill, Provost William A Smith, Treasurer James M Sinclair, Baillie James Cameron, Dean of Guild Douglas Baxter, Baillie Stewart MacLennan and Police Judge Thomas Smith. Of these, only Robbie Grigor, Bill Fraser and Stewart MacLennan survive in 2009. The late James Sinclair played a little-known, but vital role in the success of the Normandy Invasion, as the man who supervised the construction, at the Inverness foundry of Al Welders Ltd, of PLUTO, the "pipe-line under the ocean", which carried millions of gallons of fuel safely beneath the English Channel, from the south coast of England to the Normandy beach-heads. His contribution was recognised by the award of the MBE. Provost Smith was proud of having served in no fewer than three Highland regiments during the Great War, while Jimmy Cameron, although a Royal Artillery soldier in the Second War, spent much of his service time afloat as a gunner on defensively armed merchant ships. John Hill served as a wartime officer in tanks.

Alex Fridge, now 74 and living in Wellington, New Zealand, sent in a batch of photos including this one, a photo from Merkinch School and others that appear elsewhere in this publication.

He tells us: "I'm a true Merkincher and have lived in New Zealand for many years, but visit family in Inverness frequently." Alex, who was born in "The Ferry" in 1935, still works for New Zealand's Prime Minister no less. He adds: "Over the years I've had a number of jobs, including being a member of the NZ Diplomatic Protection Squad, and have had the pleasure of chauffeuring Princess Anne during one of her visits here. Before leaving Inverness, I was quite well known as a hypnotist, which made for lots of laughs at the many parties I attended. I would like to say I have enjoyed reading all the volumes of Inverness Remembered. Keep up the good work." Alex is pictured here, right, at Reelig Estate, Kirkhill, in the early 1940s, where he and his family lived after his father was taken prisoner-of-war at Dunkirk. The lad with the dark hair is his cousin Leslie, and the tiny girl between them his sister Gladys.

Members of St Mark's 1st Company, Girl Guides, are pictured here more than half a century ago on the occasion of dedication of their flags. The leaders, in the rear row, are, from left: Miss Trotter of Brin, Mary Sutherland, Rev John Graham, Cath Fraser, Muriel Graham; front row, from left: Margaret Mapplebeck, Isobel Shaw, Sybil Hossack, Elsie Macpherson, Evelyn Riddoch.

A teenage Alex Fridge joined the Queen's Own Cameron Highlanders Army Cadet Force, and was bass drummer of Inverness Army Cadet Pipe Band in 1950. He moved on to National Service with the Royal Army Service Corps. Promotion for Alex came quickly, as he's pictured here in Germany in 1955, on the left, sporting a corporal's stripes. plus a dispatch rider's breeches and boots. He hasn't identified his colleague. The truck is a Bedford QL 3-tonner, of which more than 50,000 were built as the British Army's standard medium transport vehicle between 1941 and 1945. Many soldiered on until the 1950s, when replaced by the Bedford RL 3-tonner.

A LITTLE BEYOND LIVING MEMORY

Paddle Steamers on the Caledonian Canal

The advent of steam power in the 19th Century opened up a new era of transport and communication between Inverness and Glasgow via the Caledonian Canal and the west coast sea route.

The first paddle-steamer to sail on the newly-opened northern stage of the canal was the Stirling Castle, which began to ply between Inverness and Fort Augustus in 1820.

Four years later, when the canal finally extended to Corpach, near Fort William, the Ben Nevis became the first steam-powered vessel to sail directly from Glasgow to Inverness, through the Crinan and Caledonian Canals.

Twenty years on, by which time most West Highland routes had been taken over by vessels owned by G & J Burns or David Hutcheson & Co, steamers built mainly for passengers rather than cargo began to appear on the Caledonian Canal route.

David Hutcheson bought Burns' West Highland ships in 1851, taking as partners his brother Alexander and the Burns brothers' nephew, one David MacBrayne, who became the principal driving force behind the new venture, sole owner in 1878, and remained at the helm until his death in 1806, aged 92. Some of the best-known and longest-lived Caledonian Canal vessels of the concern, renamed David MacBrayne & Co in 1879, were the Gondolier, custom-built for the canal, which plied the route between Inverness and Banavie, just east of the series of canal locks known as Neptune's Staircase, from 1866 to 1939, the Glengarry, which spent much of its 83 years' service ferrying passengers and mail between Inverness, Fort Augustus and other Loch Ness-side communities, the Cavalier, the Lochness, the Ethel and the Gairlochy.

For most of the steam era, passengers from Glasgow to Inverness, or vice versa, usually changed vessels at Banavie, being conveyed by coach between Banavie and Corpach on Loch Linnhe, or vice versa.

After the mail contract was transferred by MacBrayne from steamer to road in 1929, the Gondolier continued to ply the canal until the outbreak of war in 1939.

She met a sad end, when, after the sinking of the battleship HMS Royal Oak in Scapa Flow by the German submarine U-47, commanded by Lieutenant Commander Gunther Prien, she was requisitioned by the Admiralty, towed to Orkney and sunk as a blockship at one of the entrances to the Flow, to prevent further incursions by U-boats, pending construction of the Churchill Barriers. By that time the train, bus and motor car had largely replaced the steamer as the conveyance of convenience and choice.

The Gairlochy, pictured here leaving Muirtown Locks, was unusual in that although built in 1861, she was only bought by MacBrayne in 1894, after working the Clyde for 33 years, shortened by about 30 feet to fit the Caledonian Canal, extensively reconstructed and used on the Inverness–Banavie run from 1895 to 1919, when she caught fire at Fort Augustus. Her remains still lie in Loch Ness close to the shore. Note on the right the private "omnibus" horse-drawn carriages, which came to meet the steamers from the various hotels which owned them.

This photo of the Gondolier was taken as she called at Foyers Pier in 1888.

A paddle-steamer, probably the Gondolier, pictured leaving the canal at Fort Augustus, heading east up Loch Ness.

These private "omnibus" carriages, each belonging to one of the Highland Capital's large hotels, were pictured at Muirtown Locks, picking up passengers from an arriving paddle-steamer. Among the now vanished hotel names visible on the omnibuses are the Imperial, Caledonian, Station and Royal. The steamer journey along the canal, from Banavie, near Fort William, to Muirtown, took over seven hours.

This was how the view west along Bridge Street looked at the turn of last century, with the picturesque Suspension Bridge of 1855 in the centre of the picture. All the buildings on the left side of the photograph are long gone, the majority of them flattened in the 1960s to make way for "progress". The nearest building on the right, the old Courthouse, dating from 1789, still survives, as does the historic Gellions Hotel, though it now functions only as a pub-cum-restaurant. The business advertised as The Tweed Warehouse Arthur Medlock, has long vanished, as has MacGregor's, farther along on the same side of the street. Queen Mary's House, just beyond, then housing a prosperous wine trading concern, bit the dust in 1969, to make way for the second premises of the then rapidly-expanding Highlands and Islands Development Board, now a block of private flats. It's perhaps a pity that the Board had not been handed heritage preservation as one of its primary remits. Note the two wee boys in the picture, the one on the left barefooted, although otherwise fairly well clad, the other apparently from a relatively affluent background, the proud owner of a bicycle. Just visible, between the bridge and the buildings on the left-hand side, is part of the Columba Hotel, still happily in good shape.

Inverness Railway Station, on a sunny morning around 1910. The man in the top hat, striding down the left of the platform is stationmaster Colin Mackay, who lived at Ardconnel Terrace. The photo was contributed by his great-granddaughter, Fiona Macdonald.

This gallant officer is Captain William Macdonald of the Seaforth Highlanders, later Colonel Macdonald, photographed at Nottingham, almost certainly at the start of the Great War, by photographer A W Pierce, who like so many other photographers operating close to forces' bases, must have profited greatly from taking souvenir pictures of those heading for the conflict. The photo was contributed by Captain Macdonald's granddaughter Fiona Macdonald.

An atmospheric riverside photo taken at least a century ago, probably from the Greig Street Bridge, showing the soon to be abandoned St Columba High Church and Inverness Castle.

A photo from the mid years of last century of office bearers and members of Priory Lodge No 1235, Beauly. Can anyone tell us when this photo was taken and who those in it were – or is that a secret?

A postcard from the turn of the century, showing salmon fishing at Friars' Shott.

Thankfully the frontage of the elegant Royal Northern Infirmary, built by public subscription and opened in 1804, still survives – externally at least – largely as it was over a century ago, when this photo was taken, although the ground to the rear has been used for residential development. In those more leisurely days, the bicycle, propped up against a wall, would have been as vital a means of local transport as a car or bus of today.

Cromwell's Clock Tower is the last remaining reminder of a five-cornered fort built between 1652 and 1657 by soldiers of the Lord Protector Oliver Cromwell, reputedly at a cost of £80,000, to keep unruly Highlanders at bay, after the Roundhead invasion of Scotland in 1649. The fortifications were demolished in 1662, two years after the restoration of Charles II, and their stones recycled into other buildings, though remnants of the barracks remained for long afterwards. It is thought that the tower may actually have been built in the wake of the demolition, using stones recycled from the fort.

This view, taken from Inverness Harbour early last century by George C Gray, shows the long-demolished Citadel House, with its landmark sycamore tree, sadly also cut down at least a generation ago, to make way for "progress". Behind the house and tree is the front of the old Fever Hospital, also long vanished. The only building of this group still standing in 2009 is Cromwell's Clock Tower.

Another picture taken by George C Gray, presumably at the same time, shows in the middle foreground the small building then used as the harbourmaster's office, with immediately behind it, Citadel House, and to the right, behind the mast of a sailing vessel, the silhouette of the Fever Hospital. Note the piles of logs, then as now a staple stock-in-trade of the harbour, with apparently only horse-power to shift them, though we can see a pair of rails, presumably for goods wagons, in the foreground.

Contrast these two photos with this early aerial shot, probably from the 1930s, looking west across the town and the harbour. Citadel House had by that time been demolished, and the harbour considerably enlarged, though the remains of the Fever Hospital are still standing, and Cromwell's Clock Tower is visible in front of the fast-growing oil tank farm. Just beyond the bridges, on Maggot Green, is the Inverness factory of Lord Roberts' Workshops, a charity set up to provide work for disabled ex-servicemen in the manufacture of furniture. In the distance, right, beneath Tomnahurich Hill, the council housing estate of Dalneigh is just beginning to take shape. The back of the original photograph bears the pencilled inscription "Taken by Deane".

The sycamore tree and roof of Citadel House, seen in the earlier photo were still around when this photo of the harbour, showing a visiting tramp steamer and piles of logs on the quayside, was taken, almost certainly between the wars.

Judging from the lack of development at Dalneigh and around the private boys' school which today forms the core of Highland Council headquarters, this photograph from the top of Tomnahurich Hill was taken in the 1890s, before the advent of the short-lived bandstand at Queen's Park.

By the time this photo was taken, in the late 1920s, the new Dalneigh council housing estate, construction of which started in 1920, was just beginning to encroach on Dalneigh Farm and Queen's Park, although the bandstand in the latter was still standing. Erected in honour of Queen Victoria's diamond jubilee in 1897, it was dismantled carefully late in 1929 by local blacksmith D Mann, at a cost to the burgh council of £154, and stored carefully away. The following April, councillors agreed to re-erect it on a site between Bught House and the River Ness, but for some reason, this never came to pass, and the old site was buried by the westward march of Bruce Gardens.

A corner of the Ness Islands at the turn of last century, looking towards Island Bank Road.

Although this photo is well over a century old, many of older generations still remember when the B9006 road to Cawdor and Nairn passed through the middle of Culloden Battlefield, beside the memorial cairn, frequently causing congestion as processions of tour buses disgorged their passengers. This particular problem was solved 30 years ago when the battlefield's owner, the National Trust for Scotland, purchased over 100 acres of surrounding land from the Forestry Commission, in a bid to bring the field more into the condition in which it was at the time of the battle in 1746. The Trust also demolished a nearby bungalow and built a visitor centre, which sadly became too small to accommodate the huge number of visitors who flocked each year to the centre, and was recently demolished. The replacement centre houses a remarkable exhibition about the Jacobite risings and the battle, with extraordinary visual effects.

The caption to this unusual view, from Clegg's New Highland Album, probably of late Victorian times, states that it is Inverness from EC Tower, which almost certainly means FC or Free Church Tower. Although glass-and-concrete excrescences of the 1960s and 1970s have largely replaced the houses between St Columba High Church and the Castle, most of the buildings in the picture thankfully have survived.

Although so many photographs were taken from this viewpoint during the century for which the Suspension Bridge survived, we make no excuse for including this one, if only to show just how much of the character of old Inverness has fallen victim to relentless demolitions of the mid-20th Century, in the name of progress and redevelopment. World War II brought an unexpected reprieve for the bridge, which had been due for replacement in 1939. A temporary bridge had just been constructed prior to demolition, scheduled to start on 11th September of that year, but the declaration of war eight days before meant that the project was postponed for a further 20 years. Note also Castle Tolmie to the right of the bridge on the other side of the river, built in late Victorian times and demolished in the early 1960s to make way for a grey glass and concrete structure.

Headgear was almost compulsory when this picture, dating from late Victorian times, was taken from the end of Eastgate, looking west along High Street. No self-respecting townsman, woman or even street urchin would be seen dead without some form of head covering.

The Forbes Fountain of 1880 is prominent in this picture looking east along High Street from another popular photographic viewpoint, with behind it the YMCA building showing the Three Graces atop and the Tartan Warehouse below. On the left side of the street lies the former Bank of Scotland building, still standing in 2009, but with a different function, as has the gothic building three blocks farther on, which at that time housed MacDougall's Royal Tartan Warehouse, later the premises of the now defunct Highland Club, and currently the Highlander Hostel for young tourists on tight budgets. Note in the foreground the horse-drawn cabs for hire, rather less plentiful than the city taxis of today.

Station Square at the turn of last century remains quite similar today, apart from the 1960s makeover of the station façade. Then, as now, the vicinity of the station was the main taxi rank, though in those days not nearly so congested.

A charming summer's-day study looking north along the River Ness from Ness Walk, with the Cathedral in the foreground, left, and the Town Spire and the Castle in the middle distance, right. One wonders whether the young lady with the push-chair of a long bygone era is the mother or nanny of her young charge.

This splendidly detailed view of Inverness Cathedral and Ardross Terrace from the Castle Grounds was taken not so very long after both had been designed by Dr Alexander Ross, the burgh's most distinguished and most prolific architect of the 19th and early 20th Centuries, known as "The Christopher Wren of the North". Note how devoid of development is the area beyond the town, apart from a few scattered crofts and the former Northern Counties District Asylum at Craig Dunain in the distance. Built in 1864 the asylum was in 2000 replaced by nearby New Craigs psychiatric hospital, and while awaiting conversion to luxury flats, the B-listed building was gutted by fire in 2007, following an arson attack.

Another unusual view of the southern part of Inverness from over a century ago, taken from the top of Tomnahurich Hill, showing many buildings and features, including the rear of the Royal Northern Infirmary, its chapel (centre of photo), the premises now occupied by the Glen Mhor Hotel (light building on left) and Godsman's Walk, happily still relatively unspoiled, although the parks behind the hospital have been built on.

Man of substance and social conscience

Kenneth Macdonald, lawyer and town clerk of Inverness for 40 years, volunteer army officer and crofters' champion, was a man of many parts and quite remarkable by all contemporary accounts. Born in the burgh, of seafaring stock, in January 1850, he attended Inverness Royal Academy before being apprenticed to a local solicitor, James Anderson.

He left, aged 18, to study law at Glasgow University, where he distinguished himself by winning first prize in Scots Law and a special prize in mercantile and bankruptcy law. Besides attending law classes, he served for three years in the office of Glasgow solicitor William Lucas, whose son William later married Kenneth's only daughter Helen, known as Ella.

Kenneth returned to Inverness as a fully-qualified solicitor at age 21 and set up in practice on his own.

He and his wife Elizabeth Mackenzie, of Wester Ross stock, lived at first in High Street, in the premises now occupied by the Orange mobile phone shop, where Ella was born in 1872. In later years he lived at the mansion Beech Lawn, on Culduthel Road.

Kenneth showed promise as a lawyer, and championed several crofting communities facing eviction or extortion, including those involved in 1882 in the famous Braes dispute in Skye, when police and crofters clashed over grazings' rights.

His great-great-grandson Donald MacKechnie, from Moodiesburn, Glasgow, who provided the information and accompanying photographs, understands he went to London to plead the crofters' cause in Parliament, and received considerable newspaper publicity. This, and other disputes, led to the formation of the Napier Commission to consider crofters' grievances, and subsequently to the Crofters' Holdings (Scotland) Act of 1886, which gave crofters security of tenure.

Kenneth also championed East Sutherland crofters from Skibo before the new Crofters' Commission and those from Airdens, Bonar Bridge, in the sheriff court. In addition he represented crofters from South West Ross in their lengthy negotiations over land required for the extension of the railway line from Strome Ferry to Kyle of Lochalsh.

He served for many years in the Royal Artillery Volunteers, reaching the rank of colonel, and served long and conscientiously as a member of Inverness School Board, helping to organise continuation and technical classes.

In addition, Kenneth was a member of the Gaelic Society of Inverness and his considerable research into and writings on the burgh's history were recognised with a Fellowship of the Antiquarian Society of Scotland.

Elected to the town council in 1878, he soon became a bailie, but resigned three years later when appointed town clerk, a post he held with distinction until shortly before his death from throat cancer in 1921.

Above: Kenneth Macdonald in his formal legal attire.

Left: Kenneth Macdonald's memorial stone at Tomnahurich Cemetery.

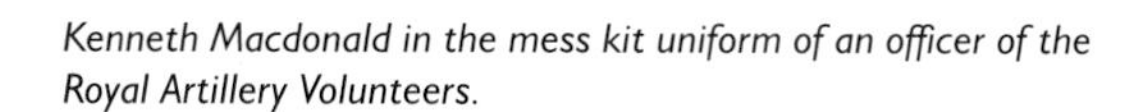
Kenneth Macdonald in the mess kit uniform of an officer of the Royal Artillery Volunteers.

Kenneth Macdonald and his wife Elizabeth in the garden of their home at Beech Lawn, Culduthel Road, in 1896, along with their daughter Ella (left), her husband William Lucas (right) and their son William Alexander Crawford Leander Macdonald Lucas, known as Leander. Sadly four years later Ella died in Kingussie from tuberculosis, leaving Leander, aged six, and a daughter Ailie, aged six months. William Lucas later remarried and went to Canada around 1910, taking Leander with him. Ailie, Donald MacKechnie's paternal grandmother, was brought up by both sets of grandparents. She died in Canada in 1988.

Ill-fated Ella Macdonald, who died from TB in September 1900, aged only 28, leaving two young motherless children.

Elizabeth Macdonald, pictured here outside Beech Lawn, with her granddaughter Ailie and a young friend. Elizabeth died in 1939, a few weeks before her 89th birthday.

We are indebted to James M Pirrie of Mackay Road for a number of very old photographs, probably dating from the 1880s, of familiar buildings or scenes in slightly unfamiliar settings. This is a rare photograph of a very new Inverness Cathedral, surrounded by a stone wall rather than the railings which had appeared before the turn of the century.

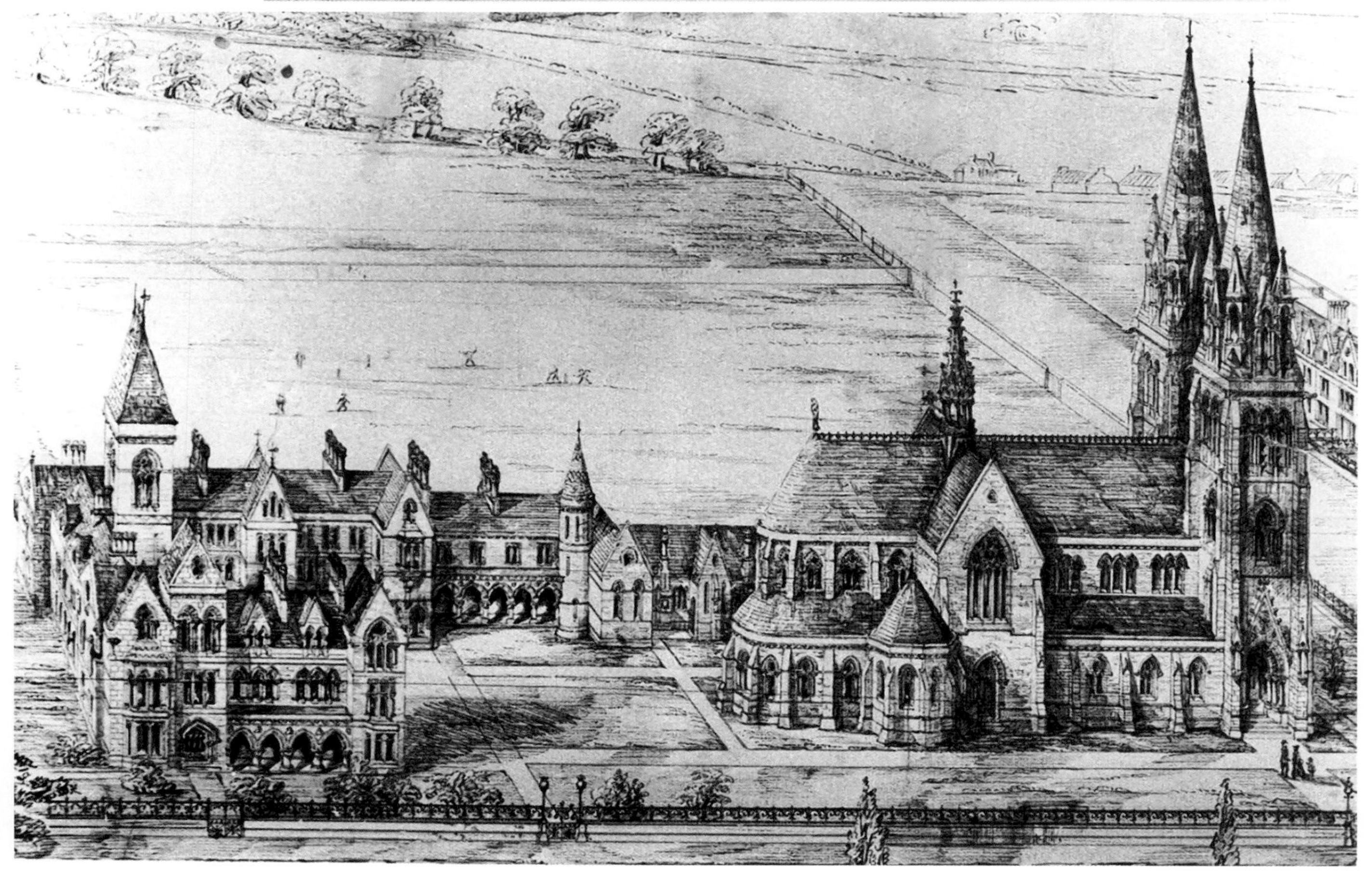

This was what Inverness Cathedral, with the 100ft spires planned by architect Alexander Ross, but never completed, the Bishop's Palace and a proposed boys' school might have looked like, had this early artist's impression, presumably dating from before its completion in 1869, come to fruition.

A view south along Church Street, from its junction with Queensgate and Fraser Street, showing in the foreground a long-vanished building in the vernacular style which housed the premises of George Macleod, Fishmonger and Poulterer. Among the adverts on the gable end are those for Symington's Coffee Essence, and the North British Railway. The building in the distance, thankfully still intact, was until relatively recently a branch of the Bank of Scotland.

Another very old view from the riverbank of a familiar scene, which like so many other photos in this issue of Inverness Remembered shows how much of the city's heritage has been lost forever.

The building in the foreground, in this view north-west along High Street, is still standing, albeit without the fancy pillars, and today does duty as a budget hotel, with shops beneath. The Town Steeple in the distance is also happily still to the fore, as are some neighbouring buildings, although they too might well have bitten the dust, had the redevelopers of the 1960s had their way.

This remarkable late Victorian photograph was taken in Church Street, looking east along the then relatively newly redeveloped Queensgate. Fortunately the block in the foreground survives largely unscathed, though the business of Christie the chemist on the corner has long vanished, as has McGillivray's Temperance Hotel, which took up much of the upper floors. The notice on MacArthur's shop in Church Street beside the entrance to Christie's, advertises Italian Ice Cream, then a particularly rare delicacy. Thanks to the wonders of the computer, we teased this image from a photocopy sent in 1993 by Alison Kennedy to solicitor Jeff Macleod, whose legal firm Macleod & MacCallum still practises in Queensgate. According to Mrs Kennedy's notes, the cabman in the foreground, right, was named Fraser, and nicknamed "Danny Cocka". The building in the distance, on the other side of Academy Street, next to the Old Academy, was Strother's House, from whence derives the street name Strothers Lane. In the middle distance is the former Post Office, erected in 1888 and demolished a mere 80 years later, to make way for an inferior glass and concrete structure. The carriage and pair in front of it is thought to belong to the Raigmore Estate.

This was a corner of the former Burgh Police Office in 1956, before the Bridge Street redevelopments of the 1960s swept aside such picturesque nooks.

This unusual photograph, sent by Mary Nicoll, of Aberdeen, shows a dairy float horse pausing at the fountain which once stood in Waterloo Place, at the north end of Academy Street, for a well-earned drink. Mary says it was taken by a friend of her mother in 1956, and that she has never seen a picture of the fountain anywhere else. The legend on the horse's cover proudly proclaims "Farmers' Dairy No 2". Does anyone recognise the young driver, over half a century on?

When did a flotilla of full-rigged barques like this last sail down the Caledonian Canal, as did these handsome vessels pictured at Muirtown Locks at some time when Queen Victoria still sat securely on the throne of Empire – or at Balmoral Castle?

TIME MOVES ON

In this postcard photo, dating from the late 1930s, a pipe band of the Queen's Own Cameron Highlanders is pictured swinging round from Ness Walk into Ardross Street, probably en route for the Northern Meeting Park.

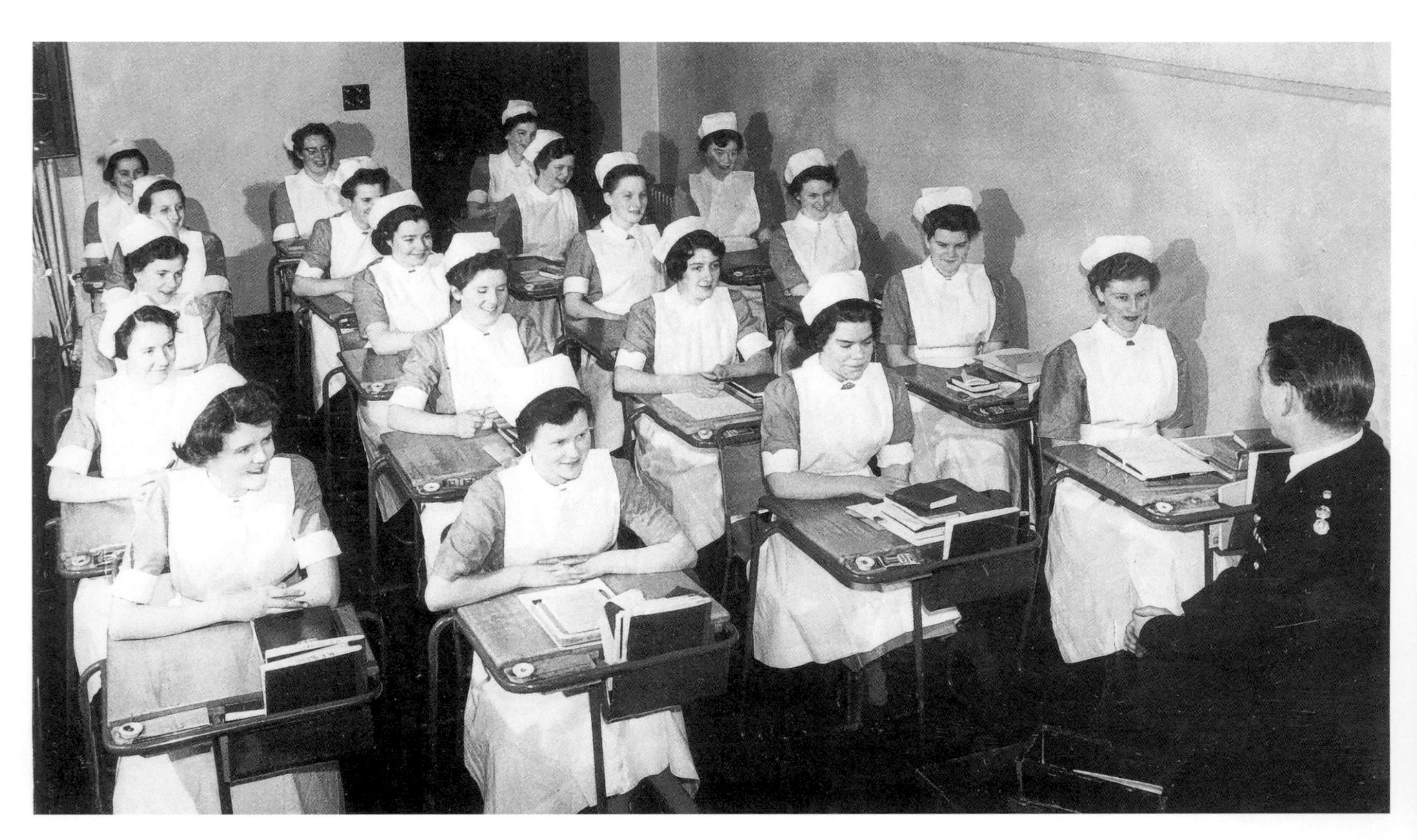

Pictured here at their desks at the Bishop's Palace, Eden Court, listening to a fire safety lecture from a senior fire officer, are members of the January 1958 intake of trainee nurses at Inverness hospitals. They lived at the Bishop's Palace, where they received three months' initial training, before being sent to the Royal Northern Infirmary and Raigmore Hospital for a further three years. This combined training course, which included a six-week spell at Culduthel Hospital, was later renamed the Central School of Nursing. The girls in the photograph, from the rear row, from left, are: Katie MacCuish, Morag Macdonald, Flora McDermid, Ann Russell, Mary Macdonald, Audrey Macdonald, Pat Watt, Kareen Bain, Catriona Bremner, Donalda Ferguson, Jean Russell, Chrissie Macdonald, Chrissie MacLean, Margaret MacDougall, Irene Wheeler, Margaret Benzie, Benny Grant, Margaret Milloy and Pat Knox.

Four railway surfacemen snapped at Culloden Moor Station in the 1940s – from left: Bill Macdonald, George Smith, Rod Beaton and Andrew Horne.

Some of the young nurses in the photograph, left, are pictured here much later at a Raigmore Orthopaedic Department dinner-dance.

It was clearly a Sunday, judging from the best suits and ties that all young men wore for the occasion in 1954, when this photo was taken at Bught Park. In the back row, from left, are: David Wallace, Donald Groat, Bill Robertson, Brian Main, Alf Macdonald; front, from left: A McInnes, Stewart MacLennan, B Fraser, Ally Chisholm, B "Grannie" Grant.

These young people, pictured in 1937, in the uniform of the Convent School, Inverness, were following a tradition that seems to have faded over the past generation – the pilgrimage to the Clootie Well, Culloden, on the first Sunday in April. They are, from left: Theresa, Beatrice, Peter and Christina Chisholm, with Mary Macfarlane.

These engineers and officials were pictured in 1984 as they inspected the Longman land renewal project, which was funded by the Government's Scottish Development Agency. Ted Murdoch is third from the left, while on the extreme right is local solicitor Kenneth MacLeod, secretary of Inverness Harbour Trust.

In early 1980 the local authority began to experiment by using old tyres filled with aggregate as a means of creating a "bund" or rampart to reclaim land from the sea beside the Longman. These photographs taken by Ted Murdoch, for many years consultant engineer to Inverness Harbour Trust, between August 1984, when work began in earnest on construction of a tyre wall, and October 1985, when it was nearing completion, demonstrate the simple, but effective technique used to create it. The lagoon created in the process was later filled in using refuse and gravel, while much of the area is currently an attractively overgrown wilderness.

Originally a church, boasting a spectacular rose window, the upper storey of this building served for many years as Stewart's Restaurant, with shops on the ground floor. When the photo on the left was taken in January 1979, the corner property was in use as a booking office for Jacobite Cruises on the Caledonian Canal, but by the time the second photo was taken, in April 1984, it was in use as a shop set up to raise funds for the National Mod, which Inverness hosted that year. The building was demolished soon after, to make way for an inoffensive modern replacement, and the rose window carefully dismantled and stored away with the promise of being installed in some other building. As far as is known, the window is still lying in storage somewhere in the city.

HM The Queen inspecting a guard of honour from Inverness Sea Cadets contingent, as she arrives ashore from the Royal Yacht Britannia to open the new Inverness Harbour extension in August 1985. Accompanying her is Colonel Sir Donald Cameron of Lochiel, Lord Lieutenant of Inverness-shire.

Ness Walk, photographed from the Castle grounds in the late 1940s, with the temporary bridge, constructed to relieve traffic on the suspension bridge, apparently closed off. Note the Columba Hotel, and two doors to the right the Ness Café, at that time owned by local restaurateurs Pietro and Linda Ferrari. Following Pietro's death in 1950, Linda bought 5 and 6 Ness Walk, the neighbouring confectioner's business owned by the Misses Ferguson, and developed the two concerns into a popular meeting place for Invernessians.

The Ness Café, pictured in 1958, in its heyday, when customers enjoyed sundaes, milk shakes and ice-cream drinks, not to mention the exotic Knickerbocker Glory. The café was a popular meeting spot for teenagers to chat over soft drinks, while members of the public could buy ice-cream cones and sliders to take away. The property today retains an Italian theme, as La Riva Restaurant. This and five subsequent photographs were passed to us by the Ferraris' daughter Leonella, now Mrs Longmore, former head of modern languages at Inverness Royal Academy, the author of several articles on the contribution of Italian immigrants to the economic and social life of Inverness, in addition to books on local castles and churches.

Mrs Longmore recalls: "The well-stocked counter of sweets, chocolates and cigarettes beside the ice-cream mixer was a focal point for customers served by my mother and my sister, Gloria Coffrini – a renowned beauty with her beehive hairstyle".

Gloria's husband Nino Coffrini was a popular figure with customers. He and Gloria later opened the Salon Continentale hairdressers at No 5 Ness Walk.

In addition to running the Ness Café and a neighbouring confectioner's shop, businesswoman Linda Ferrari also leased from Inverness Town Council the Islands Tearoom, a popular venue for visitors to the Ness Islands, especially those out walking on Sundays, or enjoying the now long-vanished open-air summer shows and dances. Here her daughter Gloria is seen in 1951, entertaining two cousins from Italy.

This smiling sextet of schoolgirls was snapped on a bright day in 1952, on the lawn of Heatherley School, a private school for girls on Culduthel Road. The young ladies in the photograph are, front, from left: Patricia Magee, Morag Mackenzie, Sheena Macleod; rear, from left: Helen-Rose Cameron, Rona Robertson, Leonella Ferrari. The huge lawn was also used for playing tennis. The school began life in 1913 as Inverness Ladies' College, in the building now known as the Glen Mhor Hotel, but moved to Heatherley two years later. Run for many years by a Miss Bedale and her sisters, it continued to function until 1956. The building, from the 1860s and now divided into flats, was designed by celebrated local architects Ross and Joass.

Bellfield Park was also used by young tennis fans, like this trio, seen relaxing close to the courts, from left: Evelyn Chambers-Hunter, Patricia Magee, Phyllis Macleod.

Fairly frequent flooding has been the curse of Inverness riverside throughout history, with the Ness occasionally overflowing its banks and bringing misery to folk living close by. The worst occurred in 1849, when the 160-year old Ness Bridge collapsed, and much of Merkinch and neighbouring areas was under water for three days. This memorable photo of the river overflowing on to Ness Walk some years ago was contributed by Win MacKenzie, of Bruce Gardens.

Mrs MacKenzie also contributed this picture of the Ness in such huge spate that it has almost reached the level of Huntly Street, which would have been a tragedy for the enthusiasts who then flocked to the Palace Bingo Hall before the new bingo premises were erected at Raigmore.

On thankfully rare occasions spectacular floods occur, as on February 6, 1989, when a particularly strong torrent, combined with exceptionally high tides, overwhelmed the Ness Railway Bridge, a five-arch stone structure built in 1862 to carry the railway north. The first arches collapsed in the morning, shortly after a train had crossed, and just before this picture was taken, while most of the remainder crumbled progressively into the river as the day wore on.

This photograph, taken just after the final collapse, by retired Inverness consultant engineer Ted Murdoch shows clearly the damage to the railway bridge.

This wartime photograph of Nairn sailor George Ralph and his wife Jean, a Peterhead lass, was taken while he was serving in the Royal Navy.
After being demobbed as a petty officer, George became head lock-keeper at Clachnaharry sea-lock on the Caledonian Canal, later moving up to Muirtown Locks until his retirement at age 65 in 1978. Sadly, he died the following year from heart trouble, believed to have been hastened by the fact that he was also the canal's diver. As a teenager he and his father received vellum certificates for their part in the gallant rescue of seamen from a Russian ship in trouble in the Moray Firth.

This advert for the Palace Hotel, from Ward, Lock & Bowden's Illustrated Guide Book to Inverness of 1896, emphasises its proximity to the steamers then plying the Caledonian Canal.

PALACE HOTEL,
INVERNESS,
FIRST CLASS FAMILY HOTEL,
(ON THE BANKS OF THE RIVER NESS).

THE PALACE HOTEL, NESS WALK.

OPPOSITE THE CASTLE, INVERNESS.

NEAREST HOTEL TO CANAL STEAMERS.
JOHN BLACK, PROPRIETOR

McALLISTER'S IMPERIAL HOTEL,

Opposite the Railway Station,

INVERNESS,

The Best Commercial Hotel in the Town.

IT HAS BEEN REDECORATED AND REFURNISHED THROUGHOUT.

FIRST-CLASS RESTAURANT AND DINING-ROOM.

ALL CHARGES STRICTLY MODERATE.

A Private Golf Course for the use of Visitors to the Hotel.

MISS McALLISTER, MANAGERESS.

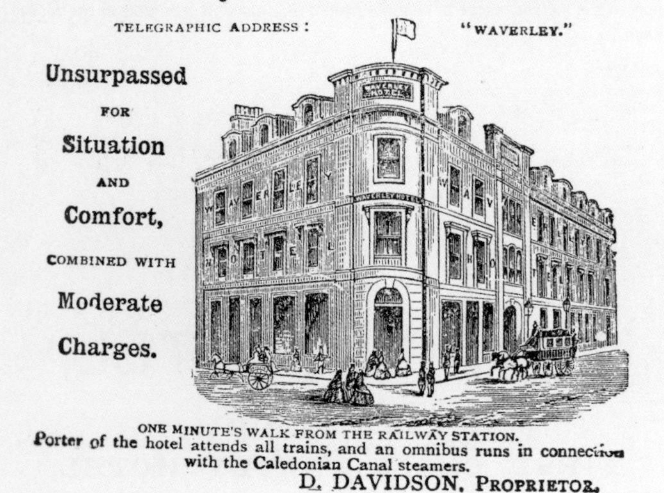

Waverley Hotel, Inverness.

TELEGRAPHIC ADDRESS: "WAVERLEY."

Unsurpassed FOR **Situation** AND **Comfort,** COMBINED WITH **Moderate Charges.**

ONE MINUTE'S WALK FROM THE RAILWAY STATION.
Porter of the hotel attends all trains, and an omnibus runs in connection with the Caledonian Canal steamers.

D. DAVIDSON, PROPRIETOR.

Also from Ward, Lock's Guide of 1896 were these two adverts for McAllister's Imperial Hotel, "Opposite the Railway Station", and the Waverley Hotel in Union Street, later known as the Douglas Hotel.

When in INVERNESS

SOUND ADVICE

Be Wise and have your Lunch and Tea at—

La Scala (Picture House) Restaurant

SURE TO BE SATISFIED.

The Rendezvous for Visitors

Conn's Tea Rooms

Inglis Street, Inverness

ORCHESTRA PLAYS DAILY.

An Ideal Place for Afternoon Tea in Beautiful Surroundings

The Playhouse (Picture House) Tea Rooms

CONN'S Confectionery Branches:
Inglis St. and Bridge St., Inverness,
Elgin, Forres, Nairn and Dingwall.

From the Ward, Lock Red Guide of 1931 – by then the Bowden name had been dropped – came this ad for the tea rooms provided by the La Scala and Playhouse Cinemas, and Conn's Tea Rooms in Inglis Street.

Of the four hotels advertised here, also in the Ward, Lock Guide of 1931, only The Gellion's remains, and even it is now only a bar and restaurant. The hotel's hospitality was praised in rhyme by Scotland's worst bad poet William Topaz McGonagall, during a 19th Century visit to Inverness. After the Queensgate Hotel burned down in 1992, the shell was reconstructed as apartments.

INVERNESS.

QUEENSGATE HOTEL

GOOD Food. Comfortable. An Attentive Staff. Running Water in all Bedrooms. Moderate Charges.

'Phone **285.** H. H. WARD, PROPRIETOR.

INVERNESS.

BUGHT PRIVATE HOTEL,

Glen Urquhart Road.

BEAUTIFULLY Situated in its Own Extensive Grounds of Fourteen Acres. On Banks of River Ness, with Access to Islands. Hot and Cold Water in Bedrooms. Electric Light. **Garage.** Officially Appointed A.A., R.S.A.C.

'Phone **514.** MISS M. MACKAY, PROPRIETRESS.

INVERNESS.

GELLION'S HOTEL

(Fully Licensed).

7, CHURCH STREET and 12, BRIDGE STREET.

Central. Comfortable. Moderate Tariff. Electric Light. GARAGE Convenience.

'Phone **648.** DAVID IRVINE, PROPRIETOR.

INVERNESS.

THE ALBERT HOTEL

EASTGATE.

High-class TOURIST & COMMERCIAL HOTEL (Licensed).

MOST Comfortably Furnished. Bedrooms fitted Hot and Cold Water. Excellent Table. Station and Garage two minutes.

'Phone **36.** JOHN HENDRY, PROPRIETOR.

INVERNESS AND NAIRN.

OFFICIAL REPAIRERS & GARAGE TO R.A.C., M.U., S.A.C., & THE TOURING CLUB OF AMERICA.

Telephone { 8 Inverness. 4 Nairn. OPEN DAY & NIGHT. Telegrams { "Dick, Inverness." "Dick, Nairn."

MACRAE & DICK, Motor Engineers, Etc.

The Largest Garage and Works and Principal Motor House in the North of Scotland.

Fleet of 30 First-class Hiring Cars.

We supply, every Season, Motor Cars, Horses & Carriages to Shooting Lodges and Visitors, **all over the North of Scotland,** from Perthshire to Caithness. Limousines, Landaulettes, Touring Cars, and Shooting Waggonettes, all Modern and Up-to-date.

Cars.—Sole Agency for Albions, Arrol-Johnstone, Overlands, and Stolwers.

Tyres.—Depôt for Michelin, Dunlop, Continental, Palmer Cord, Clincher, Goodrich, and Wood Milne.

Accessories.—Most Complete and Up-to-date Stock. Our **Repair Works** is acknowledged the **Best Equipped** in the North of Scotland.

Special Attention to Orders by Wire or 'Phone.

Telegrams :—" DICK, INVERNESS." 'Phone No. 8.

Facing matter.

The name of the motor firm advertised in the Ward, Lock Guide of 1912 remains familiar today. Macrae & Dick began as a partnership created in June 1878 between Roderick Macrae of Beauly and William Dick of Redcastle, to provide horses and horse-drawn vehicles for hire to locals and visitors to the Highlands. Over 30 years later, by the time this advert appeared, the venture had moved on to become the Highlands' largest motor company.

This family picnic photo was taken at North Kessock around 1950, when a trip across the Kessock Ferry was quite an adventure for local children. Anne Mackintosh is the baby in the photo.

There's no record of who these three young fellows are, when photographed some time between the wars. The structure behind, however, of a kind once common in British towns, but long-since consigned to municipal history by environmental bureaucracy, is noteworthy as the ornate cast-iron Victorian gents' urinal which once stood at what was the junction of Wells Street and Muirtown Street.

We're not quite sure what the occasion was when these ladies and children were photographed, but it seems to have been some sort of picnic outing. The one man in the picture, wearing a peaked cap, may well have been their bus-driver. The only thing we do know is the date, 23/6/28, scrawled on the print. Are any of the children, now in their 80s, still alive?

These three wee lassies, perched precariously on the doorstep of the old lighthouse at North Kessock, are identified on the back of the print merely as Kathleen, Isobel, Pat. The lighthouse has long been demolished, to make way for the current lifeboat station.

The man with the hat in the centre of this photo is said to be Labour's first prime minister, Lossiemouth-born James Ramsay Macdonald, centre, taken on the day in 1930 when he received the Freedom of Inverness. It certainly looks like Macdonald, but where the rooftop venue is, or who the other people are, remain a mystery.

This was the staff of an Inverness laundry, in the early part of last century. Although Linda Law, of Oldtown Road, who sent the photo in, hasn't been able to specify which laundry it is, another local history enthusiast suggests that it might be at Craig Dunain Hospital. Linda tells us that the small girl in the middle of the front row is her grandmother, Annie Mellis.

A group of Highland Railway employees, photographed in the golden age of steam, seated beside the Ben Macdhui, one of the company's best-known locomotives, which plied the Highland lines from 1899, when it was built at Inverness Lochgorm works, until long after 1923, when the Highland Railway became part of London, Midland & Scottish, and numbered it 14407. Unlike a few of its contemporaries, it did not survive until railway nationalisation in 1948. Second left in the middle row is Linda Law's grandfather, Charlie Mellis, who became foreman fitter like his father before him.

All we know about this photo of the former Millburn Distillery is that it was taken in 1923 by Chas Treasurer, Inverness, a photographer who worked in the burgh's Inglis Street. Production certainly appeared to be booming, from the number of casks on view. Sadly, little now remains of the distillery buildings, but those aspects that have survived have been incorporated into a motel and restaurant.

This photograph of Millburn Distillery dates from 1932, according to a note on the back.

The front of Millburn Distillery, also from the early 1930s, given the design of the car in the foreground.

Diriebught Burn, which flowed past the distillery.

The only information available about this photo is that it was commissioned to mark a presentation to long-serving employee, Miss Reid, probably in the 1960s. The well-tailored tall man presenting the award is a director of Scottish Malt Distillers.

The "elf'n safety" brigade hadn't been dreamed of, far less recruited, when grocer Tom Galloway was pictured enjoying a fly fag outside his shop in Hill Street over half a century ago. The site is now occupied by a barber's shop.

Members of Inverness burgh lighting department pictured taking a well-deserved rest while working at South Kessock 60 or so years ago. The inscription on the back states: "With best wishes from Johnnie, Tom, Monty, Ian and Dodoh". Which was which, and who was the sixth member?

Roll the clock back to Bridge Street, Inverness, of about 80 years ago, and you would find this comprehensive grocery business, Carrie & Company, which stood approximately on the site today occupied by Poundstretchers. Manager John Grant is pictured here with his staff, including his son Ian, the lad in long apron and short trousers standing by the pony and delivery cart, whose daughter Eleanor Mellis submitted this charming period study.

Another photo of the staff of Cooper's the grocer's shop, which in bygone days was situated at the Union Street entrance to the Victorian Market, recently occupied by Millets.

British-made cars still predominated when Rory MacLeod took this 1961 photo of Castle Street, from the path leading up to the castle. Buildings had by that time already been cleared to stabilise Castle Hill and create a car park beside the Town House. In fact the only foreign vehicle in sight is the tiny Heinkel bubble car, a short-lived fashion accessory, in front of Sinclair's furniture and antiques shop. Behind it is a sturdy Hillman Minx estate car, while in the car park are two other Rootes Group cars, an Austin van, a Ford van, a pre-war Ford and a caravan, also probably Austin. The buildings on either side of the entrance to Raining's Stairs are sadly long gone. At least Barney's shop is still there, though long under different ownership.

Policewomen were still a relatively rare breed when WPC Zena Mackenzie of Inverness Burgh Constabulary was snapped guiding children and shoppers across the busy pedestrian crossing in Academy Street on a summer day in 1961.

This picture was taken in High Street early in 1971, shortly before the British Linen Bank merged with the Bank of Scotland on March 1 of that year. The British Linen Company was established by a Royal Charter from George II in 1746, empowered to "carry on linen manufactory in all its branches". The word British in its title was a reflection of the suspicion aroused by all things Scottish after the Jacobite Rebellion of 1745. By the 1760s the company had moved into banking and begun issuing notes, while the Inverness branch was established as early as 1767. Since the recent takeover of Halifax Bank of Scotland in the wake of the financial crisis, the British Linen Bank, which here seems to embody solidity, is now no more than a footnote in the history of Lloyds Bank, having long made way for an outdoor pursuits shop and two mobile phone outlets.

A close-up, shortly before its takeover by the Bank of Scotland, of Inverness branch of the British Linen Bank, which as the legend in the windows proclaims "Established in Inverness 1767".

This atmospheric photo looking south along Church Street, submitted by Patricia Neumann, was taken from the top of the telephone exchange on a Sunday morning by her late father James Miller, a Post Office engineer and keen amateur photographer, using a Voigtlander Vito B camera, with an aperture of f11 at one twenty-fifth of a second. He took many shots of a partly vanished Inverness, carrying out all his own developing and printing. The date is not given, but the Fort Escort estate car in the foreground, and others farther along, indicate the 1950s.

A James Miller study of the Town Spire and the Castle, with the trees in leaf. The corner of Bridge Street had been cleared, indicating that it was probably taken in the spring or early summer of 1964.

This photo from Bank Street was almost certainly taken around the same time.

James Miller also took this interesting picture of Glenmoriston Smithy, probably around half-a-century ago, showing two farriers involved in a skill even then largely fading from the rural scene.

The west end of Bridge Street in 1956, before the arrival of the redevelopments of the following decades.

Engineers, turners and machine-men from the turning shop of British Rail's historic, but now long-demolished workshop, pictured around 1950.

An evening study of the Town Steeple taken from behind Castle Street in 1956.

MEMORIES OF EMPIRE AND ENTERTAINMENT

Anel Anderson was a versatile young lady, who not only worked at the box office in the former Empire Theatre, in the days when John Worth was its tenant, but also often danced and sang with Inverness Opera Company and in other shows.

She has submitted some very nostalgic pictures from the era of the Empire, which sadly was demolished nearly 40 years ago.

Pictured here are the casts, producers and other members of Inverness Marian Players, who staged three one-act plays in April 1948. Back row, from left: Nicky Quinn; John Cameron; Isabel Sharp; Andrew MacDonald; Tommy McEwan; middle row, from left: Hugh Sharkey; Hugh Lennon; Lizzie MacKenzie; Miss Aherne; Mary MacKenzie; Lexy MacLean; Mrs J Cameron; Kate MacDonald; Peter Chisholm; Arthur Sinclair; William Kelly; front row, from left: Peter Daly; Charlie Morrison; Frances Hasson; Ted Hughes; J McKenna; Dorothy McHardy; Ian Kennedy; Charlie Grimley.

The line-up for the Methodist Church Christmas Pantomime in 1944. At that time the church was in Union Street, where it was later destroyed by fire.

Above: Forty years ago these young pupils of the late Margaret Firth's dance school were captured in time at St Mary's Hall, Huntly Street, as they practised movements to the ditty ***I'm a Little Teapot****, to perform in the Empire Theatre, which was demolished shortly afterwards. Marie Maciver, who sent this photo in, says: "Third from the left is my lass Sylvia, now MacEwan, living in King's Lynn, Norfolk, and about to become a grandmother". Do any readers recognise the other children in the picture?*

Apart from being a music teacher at Millburn Academy, Anel's husband Tom Anderson was also a well-known pianist on the local entertainment scene. Tom, who sadly died in 2007, is pictured here about to conduct Inverness Opera Company in the Empire Theatre in 1968.

In this photo, Anel Anderson, left, and the late Kay Clements, tread the boards in a cabaret number in Margaret Firth's ***Merry Go Round****, at the Empire Theatre, in 1960.*

A line-up of lovelies for the summer show at the Empire Theatre in 1962 – from left, Rose Mackintosh, Rosie Macgregor, the late Margaret Firth and Anel Walton.

The Sanders Mackenzie Band playing at the Strathpeffer Pavilion – from left: Bill Clements, Billy Nelson, the late Jack Fraser, the late Tom Anderson and bandleader, the late Sanders Mackenzie.

Singer Leslie Robertson, known as Inverness's Boy Soprano, photographed when he was appearing in the Empire Theatre summer show around 1955.

The Tenerife Trio played for 18 years in the Tenerife Lounge of the Caledonian Hotel, Inverness, after the new building opened in 1967. Pictured here, from left, are Les Munro on guitar, pianist the late Tom Anderson, unidentified guest fiddler and Ted Walker on drums.

Frankie Cooper was only six years old in 1951 when he prevailed upon his dad, at the end of a music session, to hand him his button-key accordion. "I can play that tune," he claimed confidently, as his father finished ***We're no awa' tae bide awa'****. And he did, though he had never had a music lesson in his life. That was the start of a long part-time musical career for Frank, then living at 23 North Drive, Inverness. Within a couple of months he was playing with the best of them, entertaining folk at a Hallowe'en party. On Christmas morning he woke up to find a brand-new accordion at the foot of his bed and was shortly entertaining an appreciative audience of schoolmates and other children at a Christmas party.*

Fast forward to 1964, and a teenage Frank on the button-key box is accompanied by the late John Cran, from Maxwell Drive, Inverness, on drums, and John Hart, Cauldeen Road, on accordion. John Hart now lives in Carnoustie, and Frank in Kildonan Crescent, Inverness. He went on to form the Royal Stuart Combo, which was resident band in Drumossie Hotel for several years in the 1970s. The venue here was the barracks at Fort George.

It's the early 1970s and the line-up for a function is, from left: John Hart, accordion, Brian Urquhart on guitar, drummer John Steven and accordionist Frank Cooper.

Donald Dallas, better known as Dan – gym teacher, strong-man, heavyweight athlete, actor, comedian, singer, entertainer – born 1875, was one of the Highland Capital's great characters of the late Victorian era and early 20th Century. Also remembered for his majestic nose, "the nose that launched a thousand quips", he is seen in three different pictures here, playing a favourite role as Rob Roy in an amateur dramatic production in the town, in drag, and showing off his fine physique at the age of 60, although only 5ft 5in tall. Despite his lack of paper qualifications, he taught "drill" in local schools for many years, including Inverness Royal Academy. He was still alive and active in 1945, when he helped organise the first post-war Glenurquhart Games. Do any of our readers remember the year of his death?

FIRE BRIGADE SERVES

The next batch of photos was contributed by retired electrician Archie Fraser, of St Ninian Drive, and his wife Marlene.

Archie, now 74, spent his early days in May Court, served his time with a local electrical firm and joined Inverness Town Council's lighting department, where his father Alex had previously worked as a gas lamplighter. He was subsequently employed by Inverness County Council, Highland Regional Council and latterly Highland Council.

Archie's father, like most lamplighters, was also a part-time fireman, and as a youngster, Archie loved to spend some of his spare time in a garage behind the Town House in which two fire-engines were kept.

"There were no health and safety regulations then," he recalled, as he revealed how once, aged about 10, he fell asleep in the back of one of the appliances, only to waken up on the way to a major fire, which destroyed the Aviemore Hotel and tragically claimed the lives of two people.

It may have been an exciting interlude for a young chap, but on his return, Archie received the dressing down of his life from his worried parents.

In the faraway days before trunk dialling became the norm, Marlene was a telephonist at the local telephone exchange.

Ian Mellis was not only a lamplighter with Inverness Town Council's lighting department, but also, like most of his colleagues, a part-time fireman with the burgh fire brigade, and still remembered by veterans as the tallest member of the unit. He's pictured here at the scene of a fire which took place early in January 1949.

Ian Mellis is pictured here again, at the same fire, facing the camera, as he helps two colleagues. They're being watched by two young lads, who in today's safety-conscious fire-fighting regime, would probably not be allowed anywhere near the building, far less in beside the firemen. A quick scan of contemporary local newspapers failed to elicit any information about the fire.

These firemen, pictured in front of a Dennis fire engine, around 70 years ago, are believed mostly to be members of the lighting department, who doubled as local firemen. The small fire brigade, which was absorbed into the National Fire Service at the outbreak of war, and returned to the local authority in 1948, was based at Fraser Park, with an outpost at the lighting department in Castle Wynd, which survived until the early 1950s. Again, despite the lapse of time, Archie has been able to identify some of the worthies. He can't place the two sitting, front left, but the man in the centre is firemaster Andrew Don, with Duncan Macdonald second from right and Alex MacMillan right. The rear rank, from right, includes Tom Taylor, Willie Mackenzie, Alex Munro, who was janitor at Inverness Royal Academy, unidentified, Ian Mellis, unidentified, unidentified, Alex Fraser.

Most of Inverness Town Council's lamplighters doubled as members of the local fire brigade. This photo of firefighters and equipment was probably taken at the outset of war in 1939, as the entrance to the tower block beside Inverness Castle, then Inverness County Constabulary headquarters, has been sandbagged as a precaution against enemy bombs. The Dennis fire engine in the centre, registered number AST 14, was bought by the local fire brigade shortly before the war, while the vehicle on the right, ST 8119, is a Ford Model A of somewhat earlier vintage. Andrew Don had recently arrived from Falkirk to take on a dual role as lighting department superintendent and firemaster. Note the trailer hose appliance between the two vehicles. The car, presumably, was for the firemaster's use. Archie Fraser has been able to identify some of those in the photo, from left: Alex Munro, Tom Taylor, unidentified, firemaster Andrew Don, unidentified, unidentified, Ian Mellis, unidentified, Duncan Macdonald, who later became firemaster, unidentified, Alex Fraser, Willie Mackenzie, "Dot" Macbeath.

These were retained members and officers of the Northern Area Fire Brigade, pictured around 60 years ago. The lady in the photo is administrative assistant Helen Addie, while the men, not in any order, are Lewis E Byrne, William M Marwick, Duncan Macdonald, two Alex Frasers, William Stephen and Leslie Murison.

Northern Area Fire Brigade's annual ball in the Palace Hotel, 1962. Sitting, centre, is Inverness bailie, later Provost Willie "Bobo" Mackay, who was at that time also fire board chairman.

Three young firemen, pictured at the Northern Area Fire Brigade's then headquarters at Fraser Park, Inverness, in 1949. They are from left, Ian Tait, John Howie and Willie Shand, who in later years was Highland and Islands Fire Brigade firemaster.

THE BIG NIGHT OUT

Happy revellers snapped at the Post Office dance held at the Palace Hotel on February 8, 1950.

Burnett's staff dance at the Drumossie Hotel, December 1965, from left: Sally Wood, Marinna MacRae, Alan Robertson, Annette MacGregor, Cath Aitken, Derek Richardson, Helen Richardson.

Pictured at a Burns' Night dance in Burnett's Restaurant, 1966, standing, from left: Heather MacLean, Max ? Kaka Macintosh; in front, Carol Mackay.

Inverness Post Office staff dance in 1950. Douglas Taylor, of Edgemoor Park, Balloch, who submitted this photo, says there are two ex-telegram boys in the photo – himself, on the extreme right of the front row, and William Sutherland, second from the right in the second row up, with his hands on his knees. William subsequently left the Post Office on his release from National Service and joined Cheshire Constabulary. He enjoyed a distinguished police career, becoming Sir William Sutherland, chief constable of Lothian and Borders Constabulary and latterly HM Chief Inspector of Constabulary for Scotland.

We have either mislaid or not received any information about the event recorded here, which seems to be a ladies-only night out. Can any reader shed a light on the mystery?

These happy revellers were snapped at Benzies' staff dance around 1965. Sadly the well-known Union Street department store, later absorbed into the Fraser Group, went out of business several years ago, and the building is now occupied by a number of different retail firms. This, along with a number of other pictures, was passed on by Anne C Mackintosh.

Former Inverness Courier bookbinder Linda Law, nee Mellis, who submitted this photo of a staff night out, says the happy girls in the picture could be from the telephone exchange, Highland Buses or Raigmore Hospital, but regrets she can't be any more specific, apart from being able to identify her mother, Eirwen Mellis, third row, right.

These members of Inverness burgh lighting department were enjoying a night out when this photo was taken, around the early 1960s. Lighting inspector Donnie Munro is pictured front, second from left.

Few if any of the revellers in these two photographs are now to the fore to recall these happy events, although the two young schoolboys in the photo below may well have survived. Both pictures, along with many others, were submitted by reader Eleanor Mellis, who tells us that they were of staff dances held by Cooper's, the grocer's which stood at the Union Street entrance to the Victorian Market. Eleanor explains that they must have been taken before 1939, when her mother Helen Innes, the firm's cashier, who appears in both, had, as women did in those days, to resign on her marriage to Eleanor's father, Ian Grant. "She's fourth from the left in the front row in the larger picture, and third from the left in the second back row," adds Eleanor, who also points out thct the events must have been held fairly closely together, as her mother is wearing the same dress in both. Do any readers recognise any others in the photos – or do the boys recognise themselves?

These pictures were also taken at Cooper's staff dances in the 1930s. The long-defunct grocer's stood in Union Street beside the entrance to the Victorian Market. The background in the above photo appears to be the large bow window which stood over the rear entrance to the old and much-loved Caledonian Hotel, demolished in 1966.

These photographs were both taken at Emslie & Simpson's staff dance in 1973. Some of the people at the function appear in both.

Staff of Inverness electrical company B French at their annual dance around 1965 or 1966.

Members and friends of the then fledgling Inverness Girls' Pipe Band gather for a party in the early 1950s.

This picture was taken at the Palace Hotel in December 1972, as members of the former Culduthel Hospital night staff enjoyed a rare Christmas evening out.

A night out in 1968 for the staff of the former Alex Cameron & Company's store, which traded from 12-22 High Street.

Sadly F W Woolworth & Co closed its doors in Inverness for the last time in January 2009, after around eight decades as one of the town's main shopping attractions. Certainly in the store's early years, between the wars, country folk often flocked to Inverness to shop at Woolworth's, and this habit persisted until well into the 50s and even the 60s, though by that time the company had spread to some of the Highlands' other main settlements. It was still a major trader when these photographs were taken at the local branch's staff dances at the Cummings' Hotel, the first in March 1975, the second in 1984.

Veterans of Inverness Girls' Pipe Band gather in October 2005 for a reunion – rear, from left: Margaret MacReadie, Rachel Mackay, Ann Henderson, Sandra Ross, Ena Gordon nee Falconer, Evelyn MacKenzie, Kathleen McGurk, Vera Chambers, Myra Hunter, Margaret Henderson, Jean Webster, Lillian Mackay, Sheila Mackintosh, Moira Polson, Linda Gordon, Lillian Skinner; seated, front, from left: Tom MacKenzie (drumming tutor) Una Ross (widow of founder David Ross), Iris Ross.

The wee ones who enjoyed this Christmas party, held for the children of Inverness Railway Workshop, at the Haughdale Hotel in 1960.

EDUCATION DAYS

Children at Merkinch School, circa 1949, with teacher Mrs Mackenzie. Among those in the photo, are, rear row, from left: George Godsman, George Noble, Charlie Gunn, Robert Wright, J Coghill, Finlay MacGillivray, unidentified, John Beaton, A Hutchison, Iver Shanks; middle row, from left: Peter Thompson, - Christie, A MacDougall, R Stewart, M Grant, E Thompson, B Black, - MacDougall, - Gardner, S Severn; front from left: Gerty MacLean, J Rooney, Miriam Shand, Joyce Paterson, Anne Rodgers, Lydia Geddes, Mary Stewart, M MacDonald Margaret Cole, Lily Grant.

These smart-looking girls were photographed at the door of what was then known as Inverness Technical High School some time in the late 1950s.

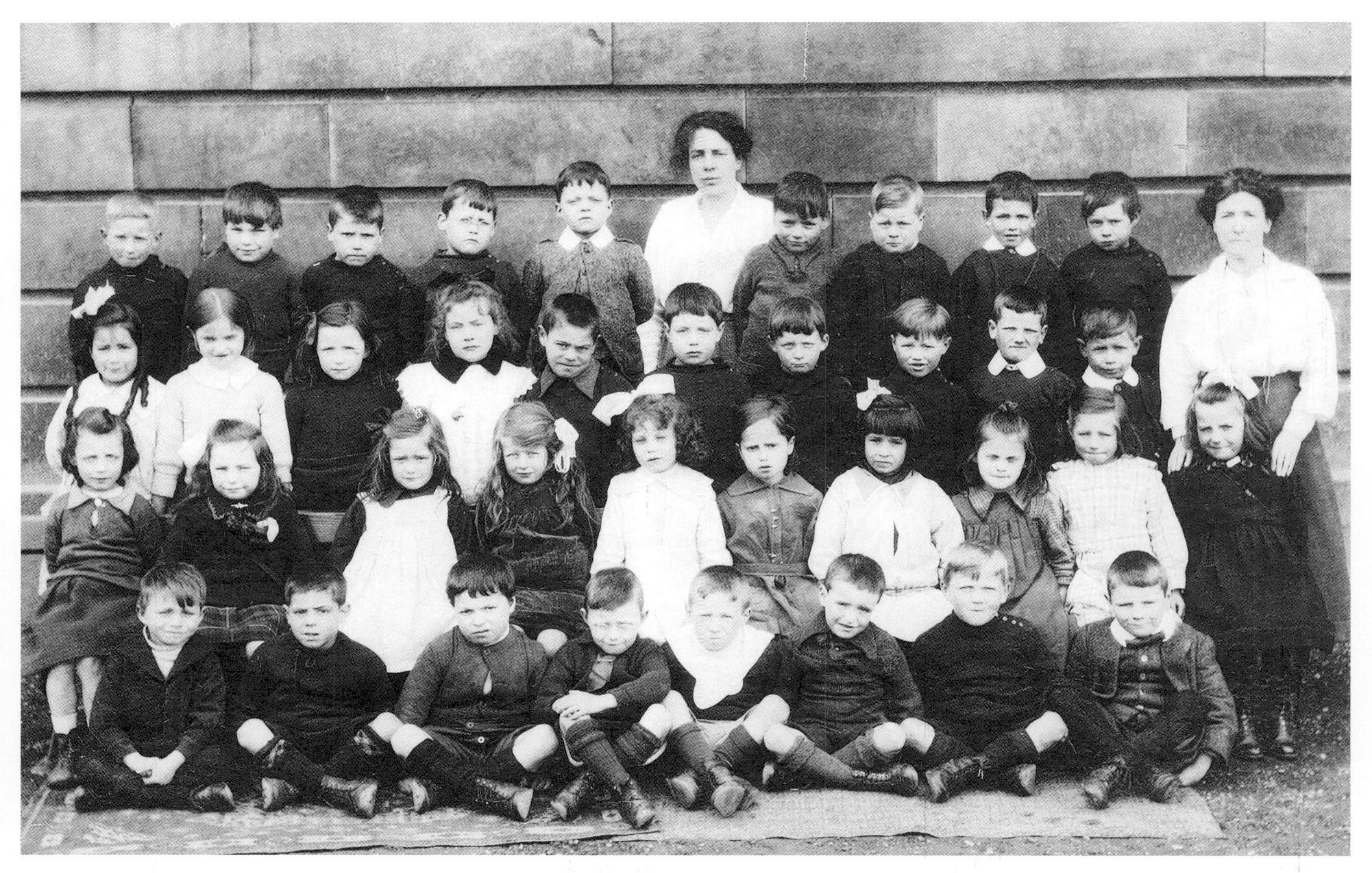

This was the infant class at Bell's School, Farraline Park, in the 1920s. The adults are head infant teacher Miss Susan Fraser and Miss Taylor, Class 3 teacher. This fine building still stands, and now fulfils the function of city library, having for some years, in the middle of last century, been the burgh police headquarters and later for a time a small theatre.

A casual snap taken at Lochardil Primary School sports in June 1980. The sturdy lad in the middle is Ronald Grant, while the boy on the right is Calum Morrison. Can anybody remind us who the other two lads in the forefront are?

Primary 7 youngsters of Balloch School play their part at the school sale of work in 1986.

Between April and June 1953, seven artistic girls from Inverness Technical High School met voluntarily on Saturday afternoons for extra tuition under art teacher James A Cameron, with the aim of painting two pictures for the school dining hall. Snapped here are four of the youthful artists with their picture of a fancy dress parade. They are, from left: Marlene MacDowell, who sent in the photo, Olive Fraser, Anna Todd and Shirley Simpson. Marlene, now Mrs Lobban, says: "Sorry I can't remember the names of the other three girls."

These two photos of staff at Merkinch School in the 1930s came from Marjory Mackenzie, of Fort Augustus. She is only able to identify her father, standing right, in the above photograph and standing left, in the one below. The bearded man below seems to be some sort of visiting dignitary, perhaps the guest speaker at a prize-giving ceremony. The pictures were taken by P Craigie Fleming, Press and General Photographer, 36 Friars' Street, Inverness, of whom little is now known, except that he was working in Stornoway around 1917 and 1918 in partnership with an R B Hackston, at The Studio, Keith Street.

The children pictured here with their teacher are thought to have been members of a class at Central Primary School in the mid-1940s.

How different the youngsters in the photo above appear from their predecessors at Central Primary School, pictured here around 1952.

These senior pupils of Central Primary School were pictured in 1962 with their teacher Daisy Ross.

These Crown School pupils, thought to be from Primary 5, were captured in time at some point in the early 1950s. The youngsters are – rear, from left: J Yuill, B Merchant, B Fraser, unidentified, unidentified, N Grant, G MacDiarmid; fourth row, from left: B McGinn, J Cantlay, D Wilson, A Macgregor; third row, from left: unidentified, E Mitchell, R Mackechnie, S Ross, W Ronald, H Macrae, J Hutchinson, F Murray; second row, from left: H Fotheringham, A Coll, N McCabe, C Duncan, E Finlay, E Grant, A Dickson, P Wilson; front, from left: H Mailer, R Macdonald, D Macintyre, unidentified, B Kane, unidentified, G Ross, B Barron.

These youngsters were pictured in the late 1940s enjoying the Crown Primary School sports and fancy dress day.

A group of girls from Inverness Royal Academy, pictured in the mid-1950s. They are, rear, from left: Joan Marshall, Janice Cumming, Joan Munro, unidentified, Eileen Bullock; front, Alyssum Fraser, Ann Davidson.

Many of these children, snapped in 1980 at Hilton Primary School, must now be proud parents themselves.

Another group from Hilton Primary School, this time taken in 1989.

These sixth year pupils were on the verge of leaving Inverness Royal Academy for the last time, to go on to further education, or to seek careers elsewhere, when photographed in 1956 with deputy rector "Pop" Frewin in front of the old academy building on Stephen's Brae. The survivors of this happy group are now in their seventies. Sadly, several have passed on.

A senior primary class photo from Merkinch School around 1947. Rear row, from left: Robert Stewart; Kenneth Mackenzie, James Nairn, William Mackie, Eric Macdonald, Jack Macleod, George Rodgers, Billy Tolmie, Walter Jeans; third row, from left: Robert Mackenzie, Alistair Dawson, Stewart Chisholm, Billy Forbes, Robin Macdonald, Kenneth MacGillivray, Alex Fridge, Angus Macdonald, Billy Robertson, John Maclennan; second row, from left; Jane Higgins, Barbara Maclean, Dorothy Craigen, Rity Nicholson, Caroline Macdonald, Mary Stewart, Lilian Gray, Rena Macbean, Mary ?, Edith Rattray, Jean McKinstry; front row, from left: Tony Simpson, James Macdonald, William Nicol, Donald Godsman, William Young, Alister Henry, unidentified.

SPORTING PROWESS

The Inverness Technical High School's Ward Trophy-winning swimming team in 1950 – from left: Brian Fergusson, Joyce Leishman, Rosemary MacGillivray, Iain Cameron.

A picture of Clach Rangers, taken some time before veteran photographer Sandy Maclaren left Inverness in 1950 to take over his family's business, Star Photos, in his native Perth. In the photo, with, standing, left, a young Clach FC supremo George Rodgers, are, rear, from left: A Simpson, C Thain, J Livingstone, J Mapplebeck, J Macintosh, C Munro, G Munro; front, from left: D MacDonald, N Webster, A Suther'and, A Wemyss, Bud Sutherland, George Sinclair.

The team from St Mary's RC Church won the Badminton Churches League Cup in 1952. Back row, from left: Unidentified; unidentified; Peter Chisholm; Doreen Hamilton; Bill Hardie; David Watson; middle row, from left: Unidentified; Hugh MacKenzie; Margaret Cameron; Frances Hasson; Tony Kennedy; Eleanor Ross; Maria Mackay; Andrew Cameron; Dorothy McHardy; Winnie Smith; front row, from left: Pat Gulley; Father David Keith; Betty Cameron; George Gordon (with cup); Frances Cameron; Nicky Macrae; Isabel Sharp.

The 1960 winners of the Standard Trophy, competed for by water polo teams from Highland District of the Scottish Amateur Swimming Association, were these super-fit young men of the LMS team. They are, rear, from left: James Robertson, Donald Skinner, coach Donald Mackay, William Allan, James Kelman; front, from left: Ronnie MacKenzie, Dennis Mackintosh, Duncan Robertson, Frank Allan.

This picture, submitted by Marjory Mackenzie of Fort Augustus, shows the trophy-winning Merkinch Primary School football team of 1932. The only person she is able to identify is her father Duncan Mackenzie, then deputy head teacher, and later headmaster at Newtonmore. Duncan, from Gairloch, won the men's gold medal at the National Mod in 1936.

Pictured with their trophies in 1972 were these Inverness Youth League under-13 winners. They include Graeme MacDonald, David Laidlaw, Allan Clark, Kevin MacDonald, John MacDonald, Paul MacDonald, Hamish Fraser, Roger Chisholm, Alec Rattray, Neil Hutton, Graeme Thomson and, we think, Steven Davidson, Geordie Thomson and Ivor Reid.

Trophy winners from Inverness Youth League 1973, B B Rovers - rear, from left: Kevin MacDonald, Peter Woolley, Mike Andrews, Paul Grant, Billy Gillespie, Roddy Innes, ?; front, from left: Roger Chisholm, Adam Stuart, Gerry Scott, Iain Clark, Ian Hamilton, Gordon MacDonald, Graeme Mackay . Kevin MacDonald went on to play for Liverpool FC and Rangers.

Over 50 years ago, Queensgate Electrical Company employed sufficient staff to be able to hold friendly football matches between journeymen and apprentices. There's no record of who won on this particular occasion, but we have been provided with most of the contestants' names - rear, from left: H Gardiner, H Munro, D Sutherland, unidentified, A Notman, A Allan, W Macdonald; middle, from left: D Mellis, P Horne, unidentified, C Macleod, W Macrae, R K Gordon, H McCombie; front, from left: K Macleod, G Jack, unidentified, J Macdonald, R Collie, N Mackenzie, A Macgregor.

The late Jimmy Grant, photographed here with his trophy, was in 1958 the first boy from the Highlands to win the Scottish Boys' Golf Championship. A member of Inverness Golf Club, he was given a civic reception in the Town House to mark his achievement.

Former Highland and Islands Fire Brigade firemaster Willie Shand, left, and his colleague and close friend Gordon Taylor, give a shoulder up to fire service control room operator Chris Menzies before they all take a dip in the old swimming pool at Glebe Street. Former wartime sailor and Normandy veteran Willie, still very fit at 84 at the time of going to print, and Gordon, an ex-Royal Marine, who died some years ago, were such experienced swimmers that they were occasionally asked to carry out searches of rivers and lochs for missing bodies, with very little in the way of safe diving equipment. Gordon, nicknamed "The Baron", was also a very fine singer.

Highland Hockey Club members meet a team from the Highland Capital's new twin city of Augsburg, Germany, for a friendly match in the early 1970s. We can't tell you who won, but it's almost certain that much beer was consumed in the aftermath.

This was Central Primary School's 1957 athletics team, pictured with the Inverness Burgh Primary Schools Shield, won at the inter-school sports. Along with headmaster Kenneth Fraser (left) and assistant head Frank Coull, are rear, from left: George Anderson, Alister Paterson, Willie Grant, Les MacDonald, Ian MacKillop; front, from left: unidentified, unidentified, Judy Munro, Harry Mackenzie, Pearl Macgregor, Margaret Brown.

Inverness Royal Academy's shinty team from 1954, with coach "Curly" Stewart, principal teacher of French – rear, from left: Alex Fraser, Duncan Kennedy, Duncan MacLennan, Duncan Michael, Seamus MacInnes, Brian Stoddart, Neil Munro; front, from left: Robbie Cameron, Finlay Macrae, Sinclair Graham, Hugh Grant, Alastair Finlayson. The young man centre, rear, from Beauly, became Sir Duncan Michael, chairman of consulting engineers the Arup Group Ltd from 1995 to 2000.

These members of Inverness Royal Academy's First Eleven, including reserves, have reason to be happy, having won the North of Scotland Schools' Cup in 1956, beating Portree High School in the final. In the picture are, rear, from left: Unidentified, Ian Guthrie, unidentified, Hugh Grant, Billy McGuire, Norman MacLennan, unidentified; front, from left: Calum Macintyre, Roddy Macpherson, Alex Fraser, team manager Frank Cunningham, Sandy MacNiven, Alastair Finlayson, Johnny Miller. Some of these young men later played for Highland League teams. Geography teacher Mr Cunningham became a professor in Vancouver, Canada.

This group was pictured at Clach Park in 1968 after the Northern Fire Brigade thrashed its Aberdeen counterpart in the final of the Scottish Fire Services' Cup. Inverness won 7-1. Rear, from left: Provost William A Smith, Robin Mackay, Bill Murray, Dougie Miller, Donnie MacLennan, Vick Fridge, George Mackay, Bill Shand, depute firemaster Willie Harper, Donald Mackay; front, from left Campbell Mackenzie, Tommy Sutherland, John Nairne, Donnie Grant, Danny Craig, Alf MacDonald, firemaster Eric Macintyre.

Railway FC were not only Inverness Welfare League champions in 1975, but went on to register a 4-3 win over Highland League club Inverness Thistle's First XI in a friendly match at Kingsmills Park on 19th July of that year. The bold lads are, rear, from left: Willie Geegan, Ally Hunter, Henry Macdonald, Charlie Crawford, Jim McCormick, Carlton Laing, Donnie Macdonald; front, from left: Paul Grant, Gary Cormack, Kenny Mackay Willie Pollock, Brian Black and Claire Rennie.

These are members of the Fourth Inverness Life Boys' football team, photographed at the Bught Park in 1948, rear from left: John Home, Iain Cameron, R Thomson, John Mackenzie, Ian Watt, Peter Douglas; front from left: Ally Chisholm, Ally Patience, Donnie Wemyss, Derek Reid, Robert Jamieson. Ally Patience, Donald Wemyss and John Home all later played for Clach and Ally Patience also played for Caledonian FC.

A group photo, taken at the closing of Fraser Park Bowling Green at the season's end in 1958.

Dorie O'Hara-Pringle
Proprietrix

OPEN: MONDAY - FRIDAY
8.30AM - 5.30PM
SATURDAY 9AM - 4PM

SPECIAL OFFERS EVERY MONTH
telephone for details

Gift vouchers available for that special present, Birthdays, Christmas, Anniversaries etc.

BECOME AN RD'S MEMBER AND RECEIVE
MOST TREATMENTS AT ½ PRICE,
telephone for details

Telephone:
01463 231091 / 232672

"The City Centre Salon"
44-48 Academy Street, Inverness IV1 1JT

Free yourself from administration worries!
For a professional service handling
Bookeeping PAYE Vat & Tax Returns
look no further than

JA Tax & Accountancy

We offer a friendly service at affordable rates and provide an initial consultation free of charge throughout the Highlands.
So relax and let us help you with all your accountancy matters.
For appointments & enquiries call **James** or **Dorie** on
01463 233755
Mobile nos: (by text only please)
James: 07774 502342 or Dorie: 07774 502343

JAMES E. PRINGLE - INSOLVENCY PRACTICIONER

JA Tax & Accountancy
44-48a Academy Street, Inverness IV1 1JT
e-mail: jataxandaccountancy@hotmail.com
tel/fax: 01463 233755

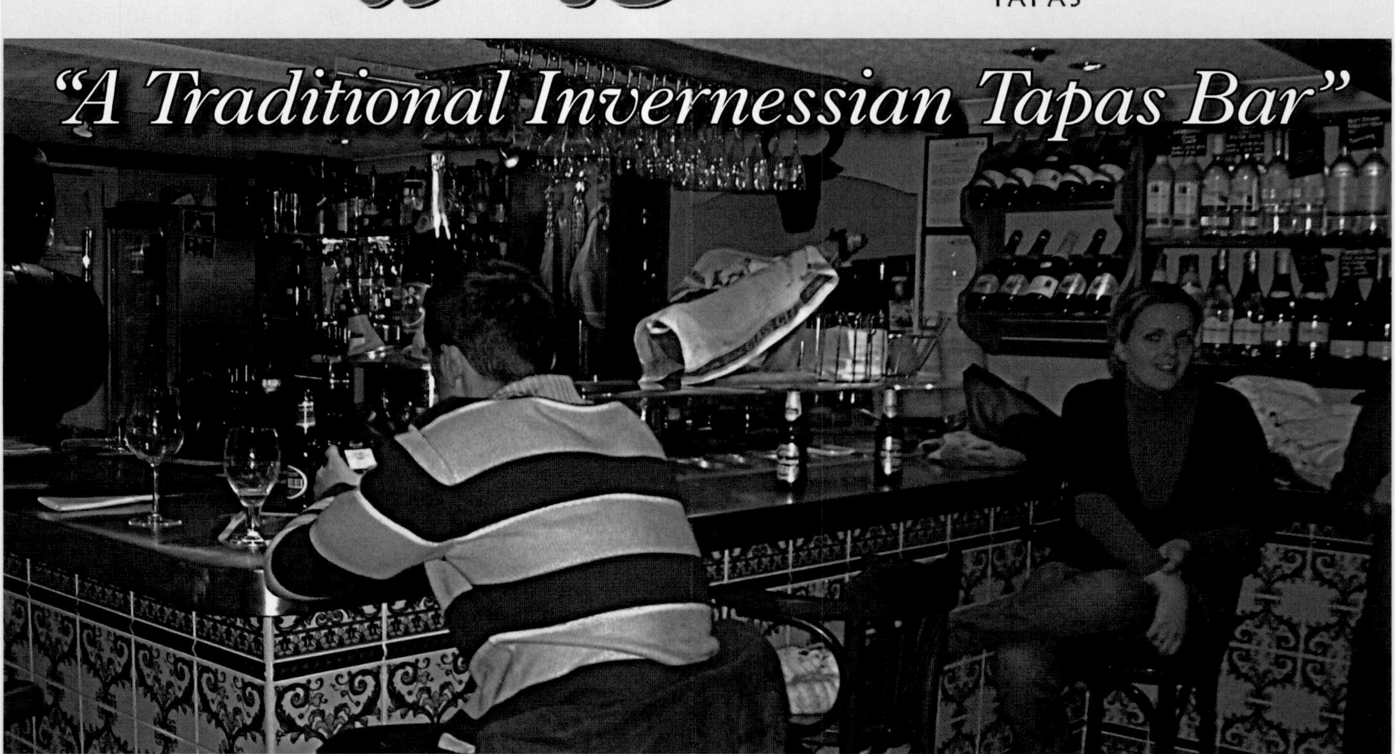

CASTLE ST. INVERNESS ★ 01463 709809 ★ info@latortillaasesina.co.uk